# I SAW GOD'S HAND

*Thrilling miracles in the South Seas*

## E.L. Martin

# APPRECIATION

To Robert Cooper and his wife, Heather, and to Dudley Houser their help and encouragement.

Published by
**Amazing Facts, Inc.**
P.O. Box 680
Frederick, MD 21701

Cover Design: Mary Rumford
Design: Allen Hrenyk/Arlene Wilson
Illustrations: Wendy Hunt

# CONTENTS

# FOREWORD

This is not just another storybook. Not if you judge the stories by the temperature of your emotional thermometer after a good exposure.

I first heard E. L. Martin tell his South Sea Island adventures to a group of about forty-five ministers and teachers—representing our worldwide work—in a crowded bus while touring in New England. I can still see him standing there with the microphone in his hand, next to the bus driver, his heart full of the subjects as his memory abundantly poured forth the almost unbelievable accounts of God's grace among amazingly primitive people. No one doubted that the practical faith of this missionary and his loyal, devoted, unselfish wife were blessed and rewarded by a miracle-working Providence. The awesome stories gripped all of us.

The highlights of the long years spent in the islands of the South Pacific as a missionary illuminated his pen, and a book has emerged that is well worth reading. The big lesson I learned from the author's life and witness for Christ was simple and moving: The day of God's miracles is not past by any means. And in the jungles of our bewildered cities and civilization we should expect to see among the people snared by the enemy similar developments.

Think of the green jungles of New Guinea and the Solomon Islands. Then think of the grim asphalt jungles of the world's cities. What happened in the savage islands among the Kukukukus and cannibals needs to happen to hundreds of thousands who are victims of sex aberrations and drugs, of crime and social disease. If God can convert whole tribes of wild natives, He can turn loose His miracle-working power upon victims of sin in the ghettos of New York, and Moscow, and Tokyo.

There is one important thing that this book says to me—that God is able to work a work in our day that needs desperately to be done.

D. A. Delafield

# PREFACE

My place of service for God for many years was in the islands of the South Pacific. What feelings of helplessness swept over me as I saw great human need, and small mission resources! But where need exists God's grace does much more prevail. In all these things I saw God's hand at work to protect and to save.

Many times during the years, as I have related experiences of the Master's leading in my life, and the definite answers to prayer, I have been asked to share these experiences with readers around the world. This I have now attempted to do.

Every experience told here is an evidence of the Master's presence. Because it is His name that is glorified, I make no apologies whatsoever. "Our confession of His faithfulness is Heaven's chosen agency for revealing Christ to the world. We are to acknowledge His grace as made known through the holy men of old; but that which will be most effectual is the testimony of our own experience." *The Ministry of Healing*, p. 100.

E. L. Martin

# ACROSS THE BAR
# ON AN OIL DRUM

When Alma and I responded to our second call to mission service, in March, 1949, our assignment was to direct the Vailala (vie-LA-la) mission station in Papua. Before the second world war we had served the Lord in the Solomon Islands. Now our home was to be on one of the world's largest islands, New Guinea, the eastern half of which was divided between British and Australian administration. It lies one hundred miles north of Australia's Cape York Peninsula.

As I will relate a little later, our early years in school at Avondale and in mission service were marked by providences that convinced us God's hand was over us continually. We expected nothing less as we undertook our new assignment. In fact, we had not even arrived at our station before God's intervention saved my life.

Crossing the Coral Sea, we arrived off Port Moresby to find weather conditions shocking, with mountainous seas crashing on the reef. To reach the Vailala District required traveling for two or three more days by a coastal trading boat, but because of the rough seas the trading boats were held up awaiting a break in the weather. (See map, p. 60.)

After two or three weeks had passed, the men at our Port Moresby headquarters, realizing the urgent need to get me to

Vailala, approached the Australian Petroleum Company (A.P.C.) with our problem. One of their forty-ton barges would have to make an urgent trip to Vailala, despite the seas, to get urgently needed drilling machinery and earth-moving equipment to the A.P.C. base inside the Vailala River. Having obtained the company's approval, our leaders asked me whether I would consider leaving my wife and family in Port Moresby and making the trip by barge. I rather hesitatingly agreed to do this—hesitating because of the seas.

In their search for oil the A.P.C. used quite a number of these forty-ton, twin-engine barges for transporting heavy equipment from one site to another, wherever their geologists and surveyors decided to establish a drilling site. These barges were usually manned by an Australian captain and about twenty local crewmen.

After about two hours' running I was told the real reason for the urgency of this trip and the reason why there was a second Australian on board our barge. We were to go first to the Laloki (lah-LAW-kee) River to install a new engine, which we had on board, in a broken-down sister barge sheltering inside the Laloki's mouth. The stranded barge was also heavily loaded with urgently needed drilling equipment.

Many, many times during the day I tried to speak to the Papuan crew but soon found that there was not one man who could speak English. My only approach to them was through the captain, who spoke the Motuan (MAW-two-an) language.

A long day's run in heavy seas brought us to the mouth of the Laloki. The captain skillfully handled the barge as we crossed a rather difficult bar. We grounded several times, but the huge waves eventually carried us over. What a relief to be inside! Or was it? For as the sun set, myriads of mosquitoes made it almost impossible to sleep.

Some days passed while the men fitted the new engine and waited for the seas to abate. Each day I walked along the beach watching the waves crash on the rocks and recoil again in shattered foam.

Late one afternoon we tuned in for the latest weather report, which suggested some lessening of the gale-force winds. With this slight encouragement the two captains decided to put out over the bar at 2 o'clock next morning, which would give them ample time to reach the Vailala bar on a king tide. (The highest tide at the time of the full moon or new moon.) The skippers asked my opinion, knowing that I had some sea experience. I answered, "I wouldn't put even the Queen Mary into seas like these."

They replied, "These barges will go through anything."

Two o'clock found the barges moving in tandem, each under its own power, of course, trying in the dark morning hours to fight their way head-on into the sea, but after half an hour's buffeting, they were forced to turn back. The seas were the master. The captains had no alternative but to wait for two or three hours and hope that by that time the seas would have subsided sufficiently for them to cross the bar. Toward 5:00 a.m. they made a second attempt in the darkness. Gradually we inched our way over the bar only to find the seas as rough as ever. The bilge pumps had to be kept running continuously to cope with the water we were shipping.

Several times during the next five or six hours as the weather worsened, the captain said to me, "Mr. Martin, I wish we had taken your advice." Even though the two barges were separated by two or three hundred yards, we could see each other less than half the time. By midday we were off the notorious Vailala River bar, known as the most treacherous on the Papuan coast line. Many a boat has met its Waterloo on the Vailala bar. Unfortunately we were two hours too early for the peak of the king tide. The captains, by signaling each other, decided to wait for the high tide and to attempt to keep the bows of the barges headed southeast with motors running at about half speed.

At about 1:00 p.m. we were somewhat relieved when we sighted the Chinampa, a rather large A.P.C. boat. Apparently it had come from the opposite direction. The Chinampa was also marking time, we gathered, waiting for the high tide to cross the Vailala bar. The captain decided to follow the Chinampa as closely as possible, for it had a much higher bridge, a decided advantage in picking the channel over the bar.

Let me pause for a moment to explain what a river bar is like. The tremendous volume of muddy and sandy waters carried by the western Papuan rivers, and particularly the Vailala, from the far-away Owen Stanley Range, carries sediment out into the sea and drops it where the river's force abates in the sea. Skippers who know this coast line could testify that often for up to three or four miles out to sea the lead line shows only one and a half to two fathoms of water (about nine to twelve feet). This depth is safe enough in a calm or nearly calm sea, or on the top of a wave, but in the trough of a wave it may be considerably less than a fathom. The muddy, sandy river waters opposing the sea seem to cause a rocking motion, thereby building a vast bar. However, the volume of water carried by the river must cut a channel through the built-up sand. This channel is continually changing and can be on the eastern side of the river's mouth, the western side, or in the center. It is seldom straight and can be the shape of the letter S or worse. A channel is seldom more than twenty to thirty yards wide, often less, and at high tide would average about one to two fathoms of water. In order to navigate the bar successfully the skipper must be able to pick the channel, almost an impossibility when big seas are running. The Vailala River is about half a mile wide at the mouth.

At about 2:00 p.m. the Chinampa began to move forward. We followed about a quarter of a mile behind and the number two barge fell in about the same distance behind us, headed for the mouth of the Vailala. Our hearts sank as we saw the Chinampa being thrown about like a cork by the

The next thing I knew I was within twenty feet of two Papuans who had been about three hundred yards away.

angry waves, rolling so heavily that the masts seemed, from our position, to touch the water first on one side, then on the other. Eventually, after a terrible battering, the Chinampa crossed the bar and we lost sight of her.

Before she had finished navigating the bar, we were in mountainous waves. The waves are always much larger on the bars than at sea. Our motors were screaming in an effort to ride the crest of a huge wave. As the wave broke, tons of water poured over the side into our barge, completely flooding one motor. Before we even had time to think of organizing some way of bailing out the water—already fifteen to eighteen inches deep the length of the barge—a second wave more than half filled it, putting out the second motor. The third wave filled it. Within moments the only part of our barge that could be seen above the water was the gate, for the barge was more or less standing upright, as the heaviest of the drilling equipment was in the aft part of the barge.

As I clung desperately to the gate, a life raft from the top of our barge washed past me. I had already tied my large expanding-type suitcase containing all my clothes, Bible, and a number of books, to the life raft while we were waiting for the top of the tide. Full forty-four-gallon drums of fuel were being washed overboard as well as empty ones. The crew members who had not already been washed overboard jumped in and attempted to swim the estimated two to three miles to land. The captain and I, after stripping off most of our clothing, were the last to dive into the angry waves. He was able to reach a second raft washed overboard, but even though I thought I was a strong swimmer, I was unable to reach a raft or even a drum. Each wave, as it broke, just rolled me over and over on the sandy bottom. Within minutes I realized I wasn't going to make it.

The nearest forty-four-gallon drum with two Papuans clinging to it was about three hundred yards from me. Between being rolled under by each wave and momentarily getting on top, I breathed out some sort of prayer, telling my Master that unless He intervened this was the end, but if He had further work for me, then only He could save me for it.

What happened during the next few moments I will never know this side of God's kingdom. The next thing I can remember was that I was within twenty feet of the two men still clinging to the drum. I clearly heard them say, "Master, try to get to this drum and hold on with us until we are washed ashore."

A little after 6:00 p.m. we reached shore just as darkness was falling. That meant we had been in the water about four hours and were washed ashore about two or three miles west of the river's mouth. I well remember lying in knee-deep water too exhausted to make the last few yards. I vaguely remember my two companions dragging me above the water line. They and I were the last three ashore.

Number two barge suffered the same fate as ours except that it turned completely over. But the Australian captain and engineer were more alert than my captain and I, for during the two hours of waiting for the top of the tide they had lashed a dozen empty forty-four-gallon drums together. When their barge was swamped, the crew, the captain, and the engineer made the shore without any real effort except to cling to the ropes binding the drums together in a sort of raft.

In the darkness we could see flashlights coming along the coast line searching for survivors. We were the last three. The Chinampa had seen that our barges were in distress and, realizing that there was little they could do with the larger boat, hastened an hour and a half upstream to the A.P.C. base to get smaller, shallow-drafted boats, lifesaving equipment, et cetera, and returned to do whatever was possible to save us. We were taken on board the Chinampa and clothed. That night I was wearing the chief geologist's shoes and the base superintendent's trousers and shirt. The Chinampa's cook had a hot meal waiting for us. Never had I tasted such delicious hot soup; it was the first food we had since the evening before. That night I was given a comfortable bed at the A.P.C. base, and I had a good breakfast the next morning.

Shortly after breakfast I asked to talk to the two men who I felt had saved my life, for in my weakened condition I was unable to hold on to the drum and they had clamped their hands over mine. The privilege was granted me. I thanked them from the depths of my heart, but it was evident I wasn't getting through to them. They did not understand a word.

An interpreter was found and again, through him, I thanked them profusely. The two Papuan crewmen, with perplexed expressions, asked through the interpreter why I wasn't speaking to them in their own language. I was quick to explain that just as they could not speak English, I could not speak their language. They replied, "No, master, we can't speak your language, but you can speak ours. From the time we told you to try to get to the drum until we were washed ashore, you spoke to us in our language."

The Australian Petroleum Company gave me a guide to show me the way through the jungle track to the Vailala mission station. I am greatly indebted to the men of the A.P.C. for their kindnesses. As far as I know, my suitcase was never seen again.

# 2

# CLOSED DOORS
# SWING OPEN

As we settled into our work at Vailala, Alma and I witnessed even more remarkable evidence of God's hand at work. Later chapters contain these stories. But first I should tell how His intervention for us had extended like a chain of sparkling jewels back to college days in Australia and before.

In my early twenties I had reached a Red Sea experience in my life, for there seemed no way back, no way around, and certainly no way through. God's demands upon me had been made clear through the preaching of Evangelist Llewellyn Jones and under the impact of the Spirit's power. I spent a night in anguished prayer feeling I had to make a decision for eternity. My whole present life was at stake.

Toward daylight I felt prepared to make a full commitment to Christ and to keep His Sabbath. This decision was to alter the whole shape of my life.

In a few days it became apparent that I would lose my job. Already I knew that my decision meant giving up movies, dance halls, card parties, and heavy smoking. In addition, my girl friend refused to follow me in my new-found faith. Now to lose my job, even though it netted a mere three dollars a week, seemed to be a crushing blow, for these were depression days. Thousands of men had packed their swags (shouldered their packs) and could be seen walking the roads in a futile search for work.

I lost my job on Friday afternoon. However, I moved forward with a slender faith based on just three verses of Scripture: "Therefore take no thought, saying, What shall we eat? ... or, Wherewithal shall we be clothed? (For after all these things do the Gentiles seek:) for your heavenly Father knoweth that ye have need of all these things. But seek ye first the kingdom of God, and his righteousness; and all these things shall be added unto you." Matthew 6:31-33.

God's promise waited only hours for fulfillment. On Sunday morning, a former partner in a sawmill venture approached me and suggested that we take over a motor business that had gone "on the rocks." His savings and mine, plus a small loan, established us in an automobile repair business.

Within a few months I learned of Australasian Missionary College (now Avondale College), and my now restless spirit longed for training that I might become an ambassador for Christ. But how could that be possible? To sell my share of the business would be an impossibility. How could my partner agree to take someone else? And who would have the money?

I prayed, and the more I prayed the more the impression deepened that I should prepare for the Master's service. In the wee hours of one morning a bright thought came into my mind. Why not pray that my partner's brother, Lester, would take over my share of the business. I tried hard to dismiss the thought. It seemed an impossibility. Lester was well established in a motor transport business some six hundred miles north, and there was not the remotest suggestion that he had any intention of leaving his business.

Praying for the will to dismiss the thought of Lester from my mind only made the impression more persistent. At last in desperation I cried out, "Lord, if You want me to go to college, then send Lester to buy my share of the business. I will take that as confirmation of Your calling."

Sleep came easily after that.

Next morning a messenger brought a telegram addressed to my partner. Surprise and consternation spread over his face as he read the contents. Then he slowly said, "Lester is coming home, but he doesn't say why." I dared not tell my partner about my prayer the night before, for he was not the least interested in religion.

Lester arrived a few days later. When I had last seen him several years before he had been a wonderful specimen of manhood. Now when I asked how he was, he turned away and filled up with tears. I dared not approach the subject. Later I learned that because of his wife's unfaithfulness his home had broken up.

Three or four seemingly endless days passed, but still there was no suggestion from Lester of his plans. At last one night when I could bear it no longer, I challenged the Master whom I had learned to love and trust concerning the reason why He had led thus far and no further. On my knees I urged Him to let me know the next day whether or not I should go to college.

Ten o'clock the next morning found me on my back under a car when Lester came in. After the usual "Good morning" he immediately asked whether he could talk to me alone in the office. Breathing a prayer, I entered the office. Lester laid his bank book on the table and said, "Have a look at that! That's all I have. Would you consider accepting that amount for your share of the business?" Even though it amounted to less than I had paid, this was obviously the Lord's leading. What could I do but accept?

While the necessary documents and transfers were prepared, I told Evangelist Jones of my college plans. He kindly but firmly rebuked me. My hopes were doomed, he said, for Australasian Missionary College had turned down a lot of applications. Furthermore, it was too late to think about college that year because the first term was half over.

My ardor should have been dampened, but it wasn't. I

told him of the Lord's leading in the disposal of the business. His reply was, "Who am I that I should stand in God's way? I'll take you over to the college. Maybe I can help you. I know the principal."

A few days later we drove the two hundred miles to the college. The principal greeted us warmly. But when Elder Jones tried to explain the reason for our visit, and that as a personal favor he wanted the principal to accept me if at all possible, the principal became most emphatic, telling us it was impossible. He had others waiting to see him and ushered us out of his office in spite of Elder Jones's seeking to explain why I should at least be given a hearing.

After some discussion in Elder Jones's car, we decided that he should now approach the principal alone. But he was unable to get beyond the door.

We again sought the Lord in prayer, asking why He had led us this far. Was this the end? Again we decided to approach the principal. We waited until there was no one else around and then knocked on the door.

The principal answered, "What! Not you fellows again!" Then, addressing my pastor, he said, "Llew, let me tell you; I am already in trouble with the fire authorities. I have too many students for the amount of fire-fighting equipment and fire escapes. It seems certain at this stage that I will have to reduce the number of students." He then added, as if for final emphasis, "I am definitely not accepting another student this year."

Then he paused and said, "Wait a bit. There is one exception and that comes from higher up than I. I will be accepting one and one only. I have the letter in my file." I only vaguely heard what he said next, for I was beginning to lose interest. "Here it is. A lad by the name of Elwyn Martin."

Whether Elder Jones knows who wrote that letter I do not know. If so, he has never chosen to tell me.

# CALL OF THE
# SOUTH SEAS

College days, while packed with interest, certainly found me with my nose to the grindstone. Study came hard, for I had been away from school for more than twelve years. Then, because of my loss in the motor garage deal and because of personal expenses for clothing and bedding, I was left with no alternative but to work my way through college as a class D student, which in those days required about thirty dollars in cash for the year. The remaining 75 percent needed to cover college fees, meals, and room could be earned by working at the college and the Sanitarium Health Food Company.

Time for both work and study was precious. If between classes I had a spare period or two, I would quickly change into my overalls, run to the factory, clock in, and begin work in the engineering shop.

I chose to enroll in the Bible worker's course, but events that first year compelled me to alter the set of my sail. Pastor Kata Ragoso (kah-tah RAHNG-go-so), from the British Solomon Islands, while in Australia for the Australasian Division committee meeting, was invited to speak at the Friday evening vespers at the college. Pastor Ragoso, whose skin was as black as my Bible, every inch of his six feet two inches a wonderful Christian, spoke English very well, but he always sensed his limitations. That Friday he came down with a heavy attack of malarial fever. He felt that by evening he would be able to take the meeting, provided an interpreter could be found so that he would not have to speak in English.

Pastor G. F. Jones, the old missionary sea captain, was sent for and urgently requested to be at the college in time for the evening vesper meeting. Pastor Jones, one of God's great men, is the only man I know of whom it could be said that he possessed the gift of tongues in the sense of using actual languages. Years before in his small boat he had made his way into Marovo Lagoon in the Solomon Islands as the first pioneer missionary. He spoke to those savage headhunters in their own language from the very moment he set foot on their soil. This made a tremendous impact upon them, for they assumed him to be one of their departed chiefs who had come back from the dead in the form of a white man to bring to them a vital message.

When Pastor Jones arrived at the college that Friday afternoon, not knowing why he had been summoned, he was asked to interpret for Pastor Ragoso, for he used to speak Marovo during the years he worked in the Solomons. He humbly explained that he would be unable to translate because he could not speak the language and had not spoken it since the day he left the Solomons. He explained that it was only as God gave him utterance that he was able to speak. This caused great concern to Pastor Ragoso who did not feel up to delivering his address in English. He finally requested that Pastor Jones at least join him on the rostrum.

When Pastor Ragoso began to speak—whether he really meant to or not I do not know—he began speaking in Marovo. Pastor Jones immediately jumped to his feet and whispered to Pastor Ragoso that he was understanding him clearly and that he would be able to interpret for him after all. During that meeting Pastor Ragoso uplifted Christ and told of the thousands of his people who were going down into Christless

I covenanted with the Lord that night to go to the Solomon Islands.

graves. A burden was placed on my heart that will never be erased this side of eternity.

Out under the stars alone that night I made a covenant with my Master to go to the Solomon Islands as soon as He called. From that very hour I felt destined to serve in the Solomons. My exuberance overshadowed my self-restraint. Soon everyone knew of my hopes. On many occasions students asked me whether any of our division leaders had asked me about going to the Solomons. Of course they had not; yet I was undaunted.

Near the end of my third college year—one year short of

graduation—an emergency developed at the home of my girl friend, Alma, in the southwestern slopes of New South Wales. Someone was needed to help harvest the wheat and oat crops for her brother, Stan, who was in the hospital with a heart condition. He was not expected to live. Alma's father was deceased. No other man appeared to be available. After securing assurance from the college that I would be able to take my exams under supervision at a later date, I left immediately and within a few days was harvesting from daylight till dark.

Shortly after the harvest was completed, word came from the college reversing the previous decision. This meant that I would have to repeat a year's work and, of course, graduation would be delayed a year. Shortly after the harvest we laid Stan to rest until the resurrection morning.

Having had little opportunity during that vacation to earn fees for college the next year, I was in a turmoil. Should I stay away from college a year in order to build up my finances? This, and repeating a year, would put my graduation forward two years.

One day soon after Stan's death, Alma's mother made me a tremendous offer, an offer that would have solved all my financial worries. Could you believe it? She offered me the freehold property, stocked with a good dairy herd, sheep, and farm machinery including a tractor for crops such as wheat, oats, and lucerne (alfalfa). There was a new house. Alma and I could have married and the place would have been ours. This fantastic offer threw me into greater turmoil than ever. What was I to do? Spend a year to try to build my finances and thereby delay my graduation? Return to college immediately and trust that in some way unknown to me the necessary funds would come when I needed them most? Or stay and take over the farm? After all, I was born and bred in western New South Wales. But if I did this, what about my covenant with the Lord to go to the Solomon Islands as soon as He called?

Alma's mother was pressing me to go into the solicitor's office on that Friday morning and have the necessary papers drawn up. She found it hard to understand why I asked for a couple of days to think it over.

Friday night found me on my knees for many hours going over the three propositions. In the early hours of the Sabbath morning I told my Lord I must know that day what I was to do—return to college, work for one year, or take over the farm. I made a full commitment to Him to do whatever His will indicated.

We attended Sabbath school in that little southwestern country town and it fell my lot to take the church service. Returning home that afternoon, still praying silently that the Master would show me His will, I was greeted by Alma's mother telling me that a letter had come in the mail. She had put it on my dressing table. Breathing a prayer, I tore open the envelope, and there was a letter from the Australasian Division asking me to connect with the Solomon Islands Mission for missionary service. I told Alma, and there on our knees we thanked the Master for such a clear-cut answer to our prayers. It would mean years of separation for us, but that would not matter as long as we were doing His will. Alma's mother still found it hard to understand why I turned down her offer.

I replied immediately to the secretary of the Australasian Division, advising him of my willingness to accept the call. In reply, he asked when I would be ready to sail. My answer was to this effect: about as long as it would take to pick up my toothbrush. However, the secretary informed me that the committee expected me to go out as a married man.

That would be impossible. My resources were too limited. My college bill was paid, but in my last term there things were close and I barely had enough money to pay a second-class train fare to Alma's home. My reply to the division made it very clear that I was quite prepared to go out alone and after a term of service (three years) I would plan to marry. The reply overwhelmed me. The division offered me wages up to six months in advance, so that we could marry and purchase whatever was necessary to equip ourselves and set up a home in the Solomons.

Alma had three weeks to prepare for our wedding. Then there was the mad rush of obtaining passports and documents and purchasing whatever was necessary, taking great care that the money was spent wisely, for after all, the money wasn't really ours.

At last we were on our way to the Solomons.

# WEDDING GIFTS
# AT CUSTOMS

Our wedding went off well and Alma and I were over-joyed by the number of wedding presents, including sufficient cash to buy a refrigerator. Although we appreciated them, the wedding gifts brought an added problem, for how could we possibly pay tithe on them? The amount was far beyond my limited resources. However, by disposing of some goods we would have liked to keep (not wedding gifts), we were able to pay the full amount of tithe.

Shortly before the boat sailed on March 19, a friend about my age but not of our faith came to me with a request. Bill handed me a letter addressed to his brother, whom I shall call James Gilmore, in the remote hope that someday I might hear of Jim. If I should, I could then mail the letter to him.

The background was this: Jim had quarreled with his mother and left home. Several years had gone by, but he had not been heard of. At the time of the mother's death some years after Jim's departure, every attempt was made to locate him, but the only ray of hope was that at one period a man by the same name had been in Fiji. I promised Bill I would be on the lookout for his brother.

We found it hard to say good-bye to our many friends and loved ones. As we sailed out of Sydney we realized that our term of service would separate us from them for at least three years.

In those days the voyage to the Solomons, a British protectorate, took almost two weeks. When we were within a few days of our destination, the passengers disembarking in the Solomons were required to fill in customs forms. We were required to declare everything in our possession for twelve months or less with the relevant purchase value. Approaching the chief purser, I asked whether I would be required to declare all our wedding gifts and our new household effects, our clothing, and so on. He replied, "Every last thing, and believe me you will pay heavy duty on all goods not manufactured in Great Britain."

I filled in pages of declarations until my head was swimming. I estimated I would have to pay about sixty dollars duty—sixty dollars that I did not have. I could see that our goods would have to be dumped.

At our first main port of call in the Solomons a customs officer came on board. He seemed to be the toughest man I had ever met. When I was paged to come to the purser's office to go through my declaration papers with him, I tried to explain that the majority of my goods were wedding gifts. He replied, "Wedding gifts or not, you will have to pay full duty on the lot, and let me assure you it is going to cost you a pretty penny."

At that moment the ship's gong summoned us to the dining saloon for the evening meal. I went, but was too sick at heart to eat much.

Sitting at the table next to ours were the captain, several of the chief officers, and the customs officer. I overheard someone at that table speak the name Mr. Gilmore. My ears were alert. But no! It couldn't be! It just couldn't be! After all, there could be any number of Gilmores who were not Bill's brother.

Some little time after the meal the public-address system

It couldn't be! From the table next to ours, where the captain and several chief officers were seated, I heard the name "Mr. Gilmore."

announced: "E. L. Martin, report to the customs officer." As I was hurrying up the steps, I caught up with the customs man and, gathering courage, asked whether his name was Mr. Gilmore. He asked what it had to do with me whether it was or not, but added, "Yes, if it gives you any satisfaction."

Calling on every ounce of courage, I said, "Not Mr. James Gilmore?"

"How silly can you be! Yes, Mr. James Gilmore."

Putting my hand inside my pocket I hurriedly produced from my wallet Bill's letter and handed it to him.

He broke the seal and, as hard a man as he was, I saw the tears trickling down his face as he said, "Do you know Bill?"

"Yes, I know him well."

"Do you know Frank?"

"Yes, I know Frank and your dad well."

In almost a whisper he said, "So Mother is dead." He asked for a few minutes to pull himself together. I stood and watched him leaning over the ship's rail and looking out into the darkness of the tropical night for about half an hour. He then turned and walked slowly in the opposite direction from the purser's office.

Some minutes later, over the air again came, "E. L. Martin, report to the customs officer." When I arrived there the customs man handed me my copy of the declarations. On each page was stamped "Exempt from duty."

"Don't I have to pay anything at all?"

"No, and don't argue with a customs officer."

From that time on Jim and I became close friends, and many times I sought his help in clearing mission goods during the years I was out there.

That night on my knees I thanked my Father for fulfilling His promise, as revealed through the prophet Malachi, that if we would bring all the tithes into the storehouse, we could prove Him, for He would open the windows of heaven and pour us out such a blessing that there would not be room enough to receive it.

# NOTHING IS TOO HARD FOR THE LORD

Because of my experience as a sawmiller and engineer, my first assignment when I arrived at Batuna (our headquarters for the Solomon Islands) was to catch up with a backlog of boat repairs and major overhauls and the installation of two new diesel engines in two of our forty-five-footers.

The sawmill was at a standstill and all over, our missionaries were delayed in their building projects, particularly at the Amyes Memorial Hospital where a large building complex had come to a halt. Then too, Mr. Singana, our Japanese boat builder, was waiting for timber for the building of the *Dundavata,* "morning light." When that was completed I had to cut the timber for another forty-five-footer, the *G. F. Jones.*

Our mission engineer was Hubert Barham. His health had broken; he was suffering with malarial fever every few days. The worry of so many boats being held up was almost killing him. My taking the load off Brother Barham's shoulders meant a lot to him. He voluntarily requested that he stay on for three months before returning to Australia permanently, so as to work with me in getting caught up.

So much work faced us that I hardly knew where to begin. Early each morning the sawmill crew and I poured out the timber from the mill. Then while the boys were stacking the timber, Brother Barham and I concentrated on the engineering. I really appreciated his help, for we certainly accomplished much during those three months.

Sleep came readily after a heavy day's toil, but one night after we had been at Batuna a week or so, I was awakened in the dead of night by a voice that seemed to say, "Jenny is in financial difficulty back at Avondale College." I got out of bed and by my bedside I told the Master that even if Jenny was in distress there was nothing that I could do, for I was still five months in the red from the advances received before we came out from Australia. Climbing back into bed, I was unable to sleep for quite a long while, for the voice seemed so vivid. Sleep came at last but apparently not for long. I again heard the voice, "Jenny is in financial difficulty."

Although my wife and I knew Jenny well, she was not a particularly close friend, and actually I knew little or nothing of her financial position and had not even thought of her after leaving college.

But the voice was so distinct, loud, and clear, that on my knees I told the Master I would try to work out some way to help. Early next morning I proceeded to the office of Pastor A. R. Barret, secretary-treasurer for the mission. I asked him whether it would be possible for him to let me have some money to send to Australia. A kindly Christian man, he reminded me that I was already well in the red. However, when I told him of the experience during the night he readily agreed to give me whatever I asked for. I did not have the courage to ask for more than $25 (more than a week's wages).

Later on in the morning Brother Barham came down to the workshop. I asked him whether he would mind delivering some money to a young woman at the college when he returned to Australia in eight or nine weeks. He assured me that he would be happy to do so. When I told him my experience during the night, he said, "Elwyn, do you mind if I add to your $25? For I always pay a second tithe, and I have some money that could be added to yours." His amount almost doubled the gift.

Some two months later we bade farewell to Brother and Sister Barham. My parting words, after thanking him for helping me to catch up on so much work, were that I wanted him somehow to get the money to Jenny, but she must never know where it came from. He agreed.

It took about two weeks for the Barhams to reach Australia, and several more weeks passed before they could get medical clearance from our Sydney Sanitarium and Hospital because of their poor health. Some three months later I received a short note from Brother Barham in which he said he had delivered the money.

Often during the weeks that ran into months and months into years I wondered whether I would ever hear the sequel to the story. When at last we returned to Australia for our furlough—and following medical clearance—I made my way to the college in case Jenny was still there. It did not take me long to find her and I cautiously quizzed her concerning her college program. Jenny replied, "Wonderful, I graduate this year! Really, though, the year you folks left was the saddest yet the most wonderful year in my life."

I asked her to tell me all about it.

Shortly after we had left for the Solomons, Jenny received a telegram from her father saying that her mother was dead and that she was to return home immediately. Apparently Jenny's mother used to work long hours cleaning bank offices and windows and taking in washing to earn sufficient money to keep her girl at college. The husband, a businessman, was bitterly opposed to Jenny and her mother. Jenny arrived home just in time to see her mother laid to rest. Her father greeted her with the words, "That's your Bible punching for you," as he pointed to the casket.

Early the next morning, the Sabbath, Jenny was awakened by her father and told that she would not be going back to college but would be working in his office; and furthermore, she would be working on Saturdays. She could forget her beliefs.

Jenny answered, "Daddy, I can't work on Sabbath."

This enraged the father, who gave her a backhander over the mouth and said, "You get dressed, have your breakfast, and I will be back in an hour or so to take you to my office." With that he stormed out of the house.

Jenny dressed as quickly as possible and hurried to nearby neighbors and told what had happened. They replied, "Jenny, we can't do much to help you, but if it would help, we will pay your fare and put you on a train back to Avondale." Looking at the clock, they found that they had barely twenty minutes to catch the train. Because she had not unpacked her suitcases, it was just a matter of closing them, and within minutes she was being hurried by car to the railway station. Within half an hour she was on her way back to the college.

Soon after Jenny arrived at the college there were all sorts of threatening letters from her father, but the greatest worry facing her now was how to meet her college fees. Within a matter of weeks the red figures began to mount until at last she was summoned to see the principal. He advised her that she must do something about halting the mounting figures.

Jenny told me that though she worked every available minute, the red figures continued to climb. Again Jenny was called to the principal's office and this time he advised her to try to get a full-time job until she could get her finances sorted out. Apparently she was unable to find employment and, of course, felt it was impossible to return home.

A few more weeks passed before the principal told Jenny that she, along with a number of other students, must sever her connection with the college until she could meet her commitments. She was to catch the school bus early next morning for whatever destination she chose.

Jenny told me how she spent the whole night weeping and praying, for she had nowhere to go. Toward daylight peace came into her soul. She threw herself on her bed exhausted and heard nothing more till mid-morning when she was again summoned to the principal's office. After hurriedly freshening up, she ran down the stairs, and as she was going out the door of the women's dormitory one of her girl friends called, "There's a letter for you in the letter rack, Jenny."

She paused for a moment to pick up the letter and within minutes was confronted with a rather stern question as to why she had not caught the bus along with the other students who left that morning.

Jenny said she burst into tears, and try as she would, she was unable to refrain from weeping brokenheartedly. The principal, a kindly man, said, "Jenny, do not feel so bad about things. Surely the Lord has a purpose for your life as He has for mine." He then suggested that they kneel in prayer together. While still on their knees the principal paused halfway through his prayer and said, "Jenny, I feel impressed to ask you what you have in your hand."

She replied, "Nothing."

The principal continued his prayer then paused again and asked, "Jenny, what have you in your hand?"

"Nothing, except this letter that I picked up on the way over to your office."

The principal suggested that she open the letter, for maybe it contained an offer for employment somewhere. With trembling hands Jenny broke the seal and there was an amount of money, not one cent more or one cent less than the amount she owed the college. After thanking a bountiful heavenly Father for His wonderful provision and arising from their knees, the principal picked up his telephone and called the manager of the Sanitarium Health Food Company, Carl Ulrich. The principal shared the experience with Brother Ulrich, after which the manager said, "If the Master would do that for Jenny, then it's about time Carl Ulrich did something. Send her down to me." Jenny was given a job as assistant secretary to Brother Ulrich, so that she was able to attend classes and earn sufficient money to meet her college commitments.

Some months later when I met Brother Barham I asked how and when he had delivered the money to Jenny. He replied, "Don't you worry about it. No one saw me deliver it. As a matter of fact, one cold wintry morning before daylight I borrowed a bicycle and rode to the college and popped the letter into the letter rack in the women's dormitory."

To me it seems evident that from the very moment Brother Barham placed the letter in the rack heavenly peace had flooded Jenny's heart, for the Master knew that we had not failed Him in our small part in His great plan.

After listening to the amazing story, I asked Jenny whether she had any idea where the money came from. She replied, "Yes, I know. I am almost positive it came from Pastor A. G. Stewart." I heartily agreed that it was just the kind of thing Pastor Stewart would do. As far as I know, Jenny still believes the money came from Pastor Stewart and I trust that she always will.

I make no secret of the fact that the whole experience put me on my knees, humbling me to the dust. To think that some three months before Jenny's crisis hour, my Master had spoken to me two thousand miles away in the Solomon Islands and in effect said, "Elwyn, if you want to have a small part in My program you had better do something." Then because I didn't have sufficient money, He impressed Brother Barham to add to mine, not making the amount less or in excess of the amount required by His child in Australia, and furthermore, sent it not a day too early or a day too late. I marvel that heaven's King, the Creator of the universe, would deign to use me, a frail child of the dust, to have just a little part in His wonderful plan.

Jenny graduated that year with flying colors and then gave a number of years of service in our work. Today she has a family of her own.

# 6

# LIKAVEKI'S FAITH AND THE PIGS

Likaveki (LEEK-ah-VECK-ee), a young man at our Batuna training school on the Marovo Lagoon, Solomon Islands, had laid down his sole right to chieftainship of Choiseul Island to follow the footsteps of the lowly Nazarene. He soon proved himself an outstanding leader of men and one who could carry heavy responsibility. He was placed in charge of the after-school-hours work program.

One morning he came to our home with the words, "Master, me like make im lik lik talk along all together boy."

We asked, "What is the trouble, Likaveki?"

"Master, he business belong me." (He wasn't in any way being insubordinate but simply saying that he thought it was something he should sort out himself.) As soon as worship was over at the beginning of school, Pastor A. W. Martin, the headmaster, said, "Likaveki, you may now say what you wish."

Likaveki stood to his full six feet and said, "Do you know, students, last night the wild pigs got in and largely destroyed all of our garden? I don't blame the pigs. Do you know why it has happened?" After a long pause, while he waited for an answer, he said, "I'll tell you why the gardens were destroyed. It is because we haven't been faithful in paying our tithe."

One boy from the island of Malaita, who had been at the school for only a few weeks, stood to his feet and said, "True. I went fishing yesterday evening and caught seventeen fish and I never paid any tithe." Then one after another stood and confessed that they had brought in their garden produce from their own private gardens and had not paid any tithe. After quite a bit of heart searching, Likaveki said, "All right, I think we can go back and plant the gardens again."

I was amazed that the pigs had been able to break into the garden, for it was completely surrounded by a heavy timber fence, but I found that the fence had been broken down in several places and that there was very little of the garden left.

The young people spent much time in strengthening the fence and replanting the garden. We felt sure that it was pigproof this time. Over the next couple of months we were delighted to see the growth in the garden and were so happy when the day came that we were able to begin digging the sweet potatoes and yams. The Lord had certainly blessed our garden.

Likaveki again came to our house early one morning and said, "Master, me like talk along all together boy."

"Likaveki, is it the pigs?"

"Master, he business belong me."

Again when worship was over, Likaveki was given the opportunity of addressing the school family. This time he said, "I couldn't be bothered wasting my time with you again. The pigs have destroyed the garden again, and you know the reason why." Then he said, "Stand up, Anasi." A boy stood up. "Stand up, Jacob." Jacob stood up. "Stand up, Limbato," and one after another he called for selected boys to stand. Then he said, "Look them over, students; there are ten standing. I am going to ask Pastor Martin for permission to take these ten boys and we will plant a garden that we will defy the pigs to touch.

After school hours were over at midday, Likaveki sought permission to take his ten boys to plant his new garden. He was given permission, but I emphasized that they would certainly have to build a stronger fence than the one that had been built around the school garden. Likaveki replied, "I am going to take those ten boys right back to the foot of the mountains where the pigs are and we'll plant a garden that we will defy the pigs to touch and we will not put a fence around it."

I explained that God expects us to do our part and then if we are faithful He will do His.

Likaveki squared his shoulders and said, "You show me in the Bible where it says about bringing all the tithes into the storehouse, and see whether God said anything about putting a fence around the gardens before He would rebuke the devourer."   I tried to explain that while the text does not say anything about a fence, we should understand that it would be necessary.

"I am not putting a fence around the garden, and the pigs will not touch it." He went on to tell that he and the ten boys had fully committed their lives to the Lord and that they were prepared to do all that He had asked them to do. They would challenge Him to do the rest.

Months went by. The rest of the students had repaired the school garden fence and had replanted it, but Likaveki, while still directing their work, had lost some of his zeal for the old school garden. Then I noticed Likaveki and his ten boys coming in each evening with their backs straining under the heavy loads they carried. Never before in the Solomons had I seen the amount and size of the produce they brought in from their mountain garden.

One morning I was busily packing our goods into cases and into one room of our house, a requirement when one is going south on furlough. Likaveki came and asked me to come for a walk with him, for he wanted to show me the

Despite the heavy fencing, the wild pigs broke through and completely destroyed the students' garden.
Likaveki knew the reason.

mountain garden. I made all sorts of excuses, for I had allowed myself the barest minimum of time for the packing and it would take at least three hours to walk out to the garden and back. Likaveki seemed hurt to think that I showed so little interest. I relented.

We walked for about an hour along a slushy track about four or five feet wide, which was well trampled by the hoofs of wild pigs that came down from the mountains at night and out onto the flats to feed on the Solomon Islanders' gardens. As I walked along that track, I was sure that it would not be possible to find one square inch where there was not a pig's hoof mark, as the whole track was a real quagmire. I was thankful that I had on high rubber boots.

I stood aghast when I saw the garden. It was the nearest thing to the Garden of Eden that I have ever seen. The taro, a native root vegetable, grew to a height level with my eyes, compared to the usual four feet. The sweet potatoes were unbelievable, with the ground bulging under each sweet potato top. Pawpaws, pineapples, bananas, in fact, all kinds of native produce, were growing prolifically and were superior to anything I had ever seen in size and quality.

I found it difficult to fight back the tears, for in my ears were ringing the words, "O ye of little faith." I walked around the garden and observed that there was no fence and that there never had been one. As I was walking around, in one corner of the garden, I found the hoof mark of a pig. I called out to Likaveki who was standing about fifty yards away, "Come over here and have a look at this." I pointed to the pig track.

"Yes, Master, but that is as far as he dared to go."

I am not prepared to say whether we should or should not fence our gardens, but I do know that the God we serve honored the faith of those eleven sons of the Solomons.

# 7

# A SON ON THE ALTAR

Alma and I were compelled to remain in Australia after a term in the Solomon Islands because of the spreading tentacles of World War II. Our fellow missionaries in the Solomons also returned to Australia. Little hope was held out for our return to mission service because all shipping and air traffic was in the hands of the Allied Forces.

I was asked to join the engineering department of the Sanitarium Health Food Company at Cooranbong where I had worked as a student during college days. This work required that I leave home early each morning, and it was unusual for me to get home before 7:00 p.m. each day. Because of this I saw little of my two children during the week except when they were asleep, but I tried to make up for this on the weekends.

Bedtime on Friday nights was a real treat for them and for me. One Friday evening after we had opened Sabbath and completed our evening meal, Leon, our two-year-old son, who was eating his last mouthful of walnuts, tripped as he ran to the bedroom where I was waiting to tell a bedtime story. He started crying, and apparently as he drew his breath several pieces of the walnut were drawn down and lodged in his windpipe.

A chubby little lad, Leon began coughing violently and coughed for hours, getting no relief. Toward midnight I telephoned a doctor, Dr. McMahon, and told him what had happened. He advised that this was a case for a specialist and urged me to get Leon to Newcastle as soon as possible. There were no trains running at that hour of the night to take us the thirty miles to Newcastle.

We were almost beside ourselves. The little lad continued coughing hour after hour, his eyes, nose, mouth, and throat swelling alarmingly. Before we could catch the train the next morning a neighbor kindly took us in his car right to the specialist. The specialist examined Leon and said, "Mr. Martin, these little people just don't get better." Then he slowly added, "To give him a sporting chance, I want your permission to operate immediately in an endeavor to recover the pieces of nut that undoubtedly have lodged in the lungs."

My wife and I were heartbroken, for we had certainly lavished all the love we had on our two babies. The operation seemed to take hours; we waited, and waited. Finally, a nurse came to tell us that the doctor wanted to talk to us as soon as he came from the operating room. He had operated through the throat opening without making an incision. He had found where walnut pieces had entered the lungs in several places. He then said sadly, "The operation was unsuccessful, so do not leave the waiting room. It will be only a matter of time."

Leon was placed in a steam tent to help him with his breathing, but by the next morning his throat had swelled so that he had difficulty in breathing at all. When the specialist was summoned to the hospital, he asked for permission to operate again. He advised us that he would have to do a tracheotomy. In doing so he would make a large incision that would enable him to get down into the lungs in a further attempt to recover the pieces of walnut.

We anxiously waited for the results of the second operation. The doctor had promised to see me as soon as he finished, but he did not. Instead he sent a nurse to tell us that the operation had been unsuccessful. The nurse added that the specialist could not face us.

The tube in Leon's throat at least made his breathing a little easier. I sat by his bedside hour after hour, but it was difficult to sit there and watch him going downhill. On Tuesday morning the doctor came and told me that on no account were we to leave the hospital, for the end could not be more than a day or so away.

My wife couldn't bear to stay long by Leon's side and watch him struggling to get his breath, so she sat in the waiting room day and night with a dear friend who stayed with her all the time. Tuesday and Tuesday night were long, weary hours. Wednesday dawned at last with little or no change in our boy's condition. Another long, weary day followed and a night that seemed never to end.

Thursday brought a marked deterioration; there was a heavy discharge coming through the breathing tube, making breathing much more difficult. At times I felt that he was gone and that the discharge had blocked the tube, but then there would be a suggestion of a cough followed by a lot of discharge. Then he would get a few breaths before having the same trouble again.

When the specialist came on Thursday he said, "This is the end. An abscess has formed on the lungs. He can't possibly go through today." But he did, and through Thursday night too. I thought every hour would be the last, for he was now fighting for each breath.

On Friday morning Leon fought on hour after hour, and now, every minute I thought would be the last. Shortly after midday, in his fight for breath somehow he dislodged the tube from his throat. He was rushed to the theater, where the specialist tried unsuccessfully once again to recover the walnut pieces. He had thought there might be a better chance because of the abscess.

After this third operation the specialist saw me and said, "Mr. Martin, we have done our best and failed. It is impossible for him to go through tonight. It's only that he is such a gallant fighter that he has lasted till now. We were right down to the lungs. They are in a shocking mess because of the abscess." He told me that he had put Leon's arms in splints so that he could not bend his arms to pull the tube out.

Needless to say, all the way through, we had been praying earnestly for the touch of the divine hand. Leon was our one and only son. I tearfully watched hour after hour expecting every minute to mark the end. About ten o'clock that Friday night the nurse who had been on special duty with Leon was about to go off duty. She picked up one of Leon's splinted arms and with tears running down her face said, "Good-bye, little man, good-bye. I've held out all the way that you would come through, but the odds have been too much." She bent over and kissed his little forehead and fled from the ward.

I had determined to stay with Leon till the end. Until he was too weak he kept saying, "Don't leave me, Daddy." I assured him that I wouldn't. Every breath was a desperate, pathetic fight, and the heavy discharge being forced out between each fighting breath caused a stench that was more than I could bear.

Falling to my knees, I said, "Father, take him quickly, please. Don't let him fight any longer. After all, he is Yours. You only lent him to us. I thank You for that." I then kissed him good-bye and left the ward. At the nursing office I left word that I was going to the waiting room and asked to be called as soon as the end came.

Hurrying to the waiting room, I found my wife and her friend Edna. As soon as they saw me they said, "Has Leon gone?"

"No, but it will be any minute now."

I asked them to come with me. I had no idea where I was

going, but I just wanted to pray. It was a cold winter night and in the dark shadows of that great hospital I prayed again. As we were still bowed, it seemed as though a bright light shone upon us. I felt impressed to ask just once more, "Dear Master, if it can be for Leon's good and for the good of Thy cause, then please put Thy hand upon him."

We returned to the waiting room and waited and waited. Eleven o'clock, twelve o'clock, one o'clock, then two o'clock, and still we hadn't been called. When we could bear it no longer I left the waiting room and returned to the ward. Before I got to the door of Leon's ward I was met by the nurse who had gone off duty at 10:00 p.m. In her hand she had a handkerchief that she had torn to ribbons.

As soon as she saw me she said, "Mr. Martin, he's coming through, he's coming through!" She then told me that she had gone to her room, but couldn't get Leon out of her mind so returned to the ward. At about 11:00 p.m. his temperature, which had been alarmingly high, dropped to normal, and the discharge stopped as though it had been cut off by a valve. Since then he had been breathing peacefully in sound sleep.

When I saw Leon it was through tear-dimmed eyes, but now not tears of sadness, for there he was sound asleep with no sign of the discharge. We learned later that a special prayer season had been called that night in the Avondale village church, and no doubt the God of heaven came very near those dear praying ones.

I am convinced that the Master let me go through the same experience as Abraham of old when He said, "Abraham, ... take now thy son, thine only son." Genesis 22:1, 2. I know I had been too selfish in praying that Leon would be healed and it was not until I made the sacrifice, saying, "Father, take him quickly. Please do not let him fight any longer," that the Lord chose to intervene. The specialist saw Leon the next morning and then told me: "Mr. Martin, don't get excited, for this is only one of the strange phenomena that happen in the medical world." He told me he was taking Leon back to the operating room to remove the tube, but said he could see no point in stitching up the wound as it could be only hours till the lung abscess would erupt again. I endeavored to assure the specialist that it would not erupt again and that Leon had been touched by the hand of the Great Physician who had never lost a case.

The specialist never sent me a bill for all those operations. When I asked for one I was told that no statement would be issued.

Leon has scarcely had a day's sickness from that day to this. Today he is a busy doctor with a large practice in the outskirts of Sydney, New South Wales.

# "IT MUST HAVE BEEN AN ANGEL"

When Alma and I and the children returned to mission service following World War II, we were assigned to the Vailala District in Papua. As I have already related in the first chapter, our arrival coincided with extremely high seas. While my family remained in Port Moresby, I went on by motor barge—courtesy of the Australian Petroleum Company—trying to reach the mouth of Vailala River. Only God's providence saved me when the barge capsized at the Vailala bar.

At length my family rejoined me at the Vailala mission station and we began our service for the Master.

A few months after our arrival our food supplies were running desperately low. The southeast season seemed to be at its worst. On the coast of Western Papua boats were sheltering in the only haven as the seas crashed on the shore line. We had anxiously waited for a six-month grocery order from Sydney, Australia. In those days we received mail only about every four to six weeks.

When goods were cleared through customs in Port Moresby they were then brought by coastal trading boats to a landing place about five miles from our mission station, which was one hundred and fifty miles northwest of Port Moresby. In order to reach the landing place, known as Maira (My-rah)

coconut plantation, coastal boats had to cross the notorious
Vailala River bar. (See map, p. 60.)

There was a lull in the weather and one coastal boat was
able to cross the bar. We rejoiced, for soon we would be
enjoying good meals again, including fresh homemade bread.
We had been out of flour for weeks. But our rejoicing was
short-lived. A shipping strike had prevented our grocery
order's being shipped from Sydney.

We had no alternative but to order supplies from Port
Moresby. However, there was one glimmer of hope. Another
coastal boat was to call in two weeks at the next king tide to
catch up on the backlog of copra waiting to be shipped from
Maira Plantation. Many prayers ascended to Heaven as we
tried to stretch our meager supplies, supplementing them with
local foods, which we still found unpalatable.

Two weeks went by, but on each day of those two weeks
the sea seemed to increase its fury. No boats ventured out of
their protecting harbors. This meant that it would be at least
two more weeks before another boat could come—weather
permitting.

Our concern increased as we saw our children—now
four in number—rapidly losing weight, for their stomachs
could not digest the native foods. By the time the next coastal
boat was due we were down to two tins of food, a one-pound
tin each of cauliflower and marmalade jam.

Seas were still rough but perhaps had abated a little, so I
summoned the national teachers on the mission station to my
house on Thursday evening for a prayer season. They already
knew of our desperate plight. Earnest prayers ascended that
night, for we knew that our extremity is God's opportunity.
We retired that night with the assurance that our prayers were
soon to be answered. For the next three days favorable high
tides were due.

The next morning, Friday, excitement mounted, for a
runner came through from the coast to tell us that a coastal

boat was approaching the Vailala bar. Our mission station was about five miles inland from the Maira Plantation and the same distance from the coast.

I left our mission station immediately with twelve stalwart students to walk one and a half hours to the landing at Maira Plantation. Our pathway through the heavy jungle was a single-file track, but the boys would be able to carry sufficient food for Sabbath. We were somewhat disappointed that the boat had not yet reached the landing place. We sat down to wait. We waited and waited while the hours slipped slowly by. Then another runner came through to say that the seas were too rough for the boat to cross the bar and that it had apparently returned to Yule Island, which was several hours away and the only real shelter on that stretch of coast line.

As we turned with heavy hearts to walk back, I suggested that we should kneel right there in that jungle setting and acknowledge that we would still trust Him although we could not understand. Rising from our knees, we were met by the plantation manager, a fine man to whom I had given two sheets of arc-mesh some few weeks before for the purpose of making a fish trap. I paused for a moment to greet him and to ask whether the fish trap was a success.

The plantation manager informed me that until the southeast season had really set in with its torrential rains he used to pull fish out of the trap several times each week. He went on to say that for the past few weeks the Vailala had been in flood and he hadn't caught any fish.

I said, "Let's pull the trap out of the river just in case there're fish in it."

"I pulled it out of the water this morning," he replied, "and there was nothing. The trap is not even set now. You can see the top of it above the water near the wharf."

The fish trap was cylindrical, about eight feet long and three feet in diameter, with a cone-shaped entrance at each end. Apparently when placed horizontally in the water, it was

Returning to the mission station without the sorely
needed provisions, I saw a beautiful Papuan woman
standing by a side trail. "Master, I have a gift," she said
in the Motuan language.

an effective trap. However, the trap was now standing vertically with about one foot protruding above the muddy waters
of the Vailala. We bade farewell to the manager and again
started off. After about a hundred yards I was overwhelmingly impressed to turn back. I hesitated, then taking my
courage in both hands, asked the manager whether I could
pull his trap out of the water.

"Yes, pull it out if you want to see how it is made. I'll
give you all that is in it."

Sheepishly I asked my boys to help me pull the trap up
onto the wharf by the strong ropes attached to it. Imagine our
surprise to find in that trap a large burramundi (clean fish)
weighing just over twenty-five pounds.

The manager was dumfounded. How would it be possible for a fish to get into that trap unless it was airborne and
then dived vertically into the trap? I felt I knew how the fish
got into that trap. I wondered then whether my wife would
cook it if we carried it back to the mission. No flesh foods
had crossed our table for years.

The fish was tied to a pole. With one of the boys carrying each end, we set off. Six boys walked in front of me, two
of them carrying the fish, and six boys behind.

About halfway back to the mission another narrow pathway led off our track. Standing right on the edge of our track,
where the other track veered off, stood a beautiful Papuan
woman. I was deeply impressed with her lovely face and in
memory I can still see her standing there.

Turning to me, she spoke in the Motuan language. The
equivalent in English would be "Master, I have a gift for
you."

I thanked her and asked her what it was.

"You see."

Turning to my boys, I said, "Please see what that woman's
gift is for me."

The boys in chorus said, "Master, there is no woman."

Impatiently I said, "The woman who just spoke to me."

"Master, no woman spoke to you."

It is not to my credit to say so, but I said, "You clowns, the woman who is standing there," but when I turned, she was gone. How I regretted speaking those hasty words!

Where the woman had been standing was a wheat sack, uncommon in those outback areas. Opening the sack, we found it to be well over half full of beautiful yellow yams (a root vegetable something like a sweet potato). Do you know that type of yam could not be grown within many days' walking distance of our area?

The boys hastily tied the bag to a pole. Again, one carrying each end, we set off for home. I found it hard to fight back the tears as I listened to the conversation of my boys as we walked back. Over and over again I heard words such as these, "It must have been an angel," and, "Why weren't we permitted to see the angel or at least hear the angel speak? Is it because our skins are black and he is white?" I assured them that it would not be because of the difference in skin color.

Upon our arrival at the mission station I telephoned my wife. Our house, on the top of a small hill about three hundred yards away, overlooked the mission compound. I could hear my wife crying over the telephone as I told her that the boat had been unable to cross the bar. I then asked, "If I were to bring home a fish, would you cook it?"

She replied, "Yes, scales and all."

For our Friday evening meal we had fish and yams. For breakfast on Sabbath, yams and fish; for lunch, fish and yams; for the evening meal, yams and fish; and for breakfast the next morning the same. Shortly after breakfast a runner came through from the coast to tell us that a boat had just crossed the bar—a boat carrying our needed supplies.

I agree wholeheartedly with my boys. It must have been an angel. But the thing that put me on my knees was the fact that the heavenly being with her beautiful face deigned to call me "Master."

# THE DEVIL'S SPELL
# ON OVEKE

To our surprise one day we had a rather singular request made of us. A young man about twenty years of age from along the weather coast asked to be admitted as a student in the mission school. With the school year well under way, we already had more students than our budget allowed. But after careful consideration I told him that we would permit him to stay. One reason was that he was our first student from his village, which was known as one of the hotbeds of *puri puri* (POOR-ee POOR-ee), devilism similar to pointing the bone among the Australian aborigines.

Let it be known here that I have seen strong young men, perhaps in the eighteen- to twenty-five-year bracket, who were marked to die when in apparently perfect health. Generally when they are marked to die they are told that they will be dead by sunset the following day, and try as you might, you are unable to save them, unless you have been in contact with them long enough to instill in their minds the conviction that the devil's power doesn't compare with the power of God. This instruction is useless after they are marked to die. It generally takes several weeks and more often many months of exposure to Christian truth. I have seen many a young man marked to die and have done all I could to save him, only to watch him die within twenty-four to thirty-six hours.

The young man, Oveke (AW-veck-ee) by name, was at our school only a few days when I was informed that some of his village folk had come to advise him that he should return home immediately, otherwise his father would puri puri him. I did not know till then that his father was a devil priest of a vast area. Oveke refused to go. I was fearful for his safety. During those few days I had spent much time trying to get him to understand that the Master I served was vastly superior to the devil, and that when in need all he had to do was to speak the name of Jesus.

Oveke told me that his father wanted him to follow him in his lucrative business. A devil priest can demand almost any price from a man who has an enemy whom he wants put to death.

Just a day or so later, on the Sabbath, when we came out from the church service, one of my students whispered that the puri puri man was on the mission station. I hurried to find him, but when he saw me he fled before I could even speak to him. I was almost sure that he hadn't been close to Oveke so was somewhat relieved. It is not actually necessary for the devil priest to touch his victim, but he must come close or have some of his devil charms carried from him to his victim by one of his cohorts.

When we closed the Sabbath I was informed that the devil priest was again on the mission compound. Again he evaded me.

About an hour and a half after Sabbath, as we were having our evening meal, one of the students told me to come quickly. Oveke was dying. It took me some minutes to get the story from the agitated and breathless student. I ran every step of the way down the hill to the mission compound. There was Oveke with froth and blood coming out of his mouth and nose; he was being thrown about in a kind of convulsion. Several of the boys were trying to hold him down, some of them much bigger than he, but he just sent them spinning. A dozen of them had no success holding him down.

I asked what had happened and was told by students and teachers alike that soon after I had returned to my house after closing the Sabbath, Oveke was thrown on the ground and began speaking in some unknown tongue. Before someone was able to run for me Oveke had disappeared but reappeared about twenty minutes later. Again he was thrown on the ground and he called out in a tongue that no one could understand. Someone started running for me, but again Oveke seemed to vanish into thin air, only to return again in twenty minutes in as mysterious a manner as he had disappeared. Then he was gone again after being violently thrown about on the ground. It seems that his fourth reappearance coincided with my arrival.

As soon as I was able to catch my breath and sum up the situation, I realized that Oveke was possessed by a devil or devils similar to the man spoken of in the fifth chapter of Mark.

I called the teachers together and we knelt in prayer. Each prayed. All the time we were praying we could hear Oveke being thrown around and shouting out the name of the devil priest and then rambling off into some unknown tongue. We pleaded with the Lord to grant us victory over the demon. At last we arose from our knees, knowing that if asked we would have to admit defeat. Then in desperation I cried out above the shrieks of Oveke, "I command you in the name of the Lord Jesus Christ to come out of him!" Immediately Oveke was thrown to the ground and was calm.

Completely exhausted, Oveke lay there bruised and bleeding freely from injuries he had received when being so violently thrown about. I put my arms around him and waited for him to gain his breath. He then told me that he had been down to the Maira Plantation three times since sunset. Maira was five miles away and it would have taken at least an hour and a half to walk the distance at night. Walking was the only means of travel. Oveke claimed he had been there three times in a little more than an hour. This just didn't make sense, but then my students and teachers testified to the fact that he had been there and had disappeared, reappeared and gone again, only to reappear and vanish again. They had already said in chorus, "This is the fourth time he has returned."

Oveke made a good recovery and maintained excellent progress at our mission school but lived in constant fear of what might happen to him. However, he soon made a full commitment to Christ and from then on his fears left him.

I should pause to mention that I later asked Oveke why he not spoken the name of Jesus during his seizure. He explained that he had tried to speak the Master's name, but every time as he tried he spoke his father's name.

One day some three weeks later I was down at the Maira Plantation and was approached by the manager. "Mr. Martin, we had a frightening experience here one Saturday night about three weeks ago." He told me how his boss boy had run to the house asking him to come quickly for there was a madman frightening the labor (about one hundred Papuans employed on the plantation) by shouting at them in a language they could not understand. The manager told me that by the time he got there the "madman" was gone.

According to the manager, he had no sooner returned to his home and settled down to the book he was reading when the boss boy shouted, "Master, come quickly, the madman is here again." This time the manager threatened the boss boy that if he went over and there was no one there he would punish him. The manager hurried over again to find that the intruder had gone. But he did not punish the boss boy, for he and the rest of the labor line were already too distressed.

He returned to his home, but before he was able to settle down the shout went up again, "The madman is here." This time the manager picked up a firearm and ran to the laborers' quarters to be told that the madman had gone again. The manager completed his story by saying, "Work that one out and tell me the answer."

I asked him whether he had any idea who the madman was. He replied, "Not really. My boys claim it was a boy by the name of Oveke who finished his two-year contract with me a few weeks ago. But I am certain it wasn't Oveke, for he was one of the best boys I ever had. Besides, he could speak only two languages, both well known to my boys and me."

I can only repeat the manager's request, "Work that one out and tell me the answer."

Even though Oveke gained the victory through Christ, I was soon to learn that the devil had not finished with me.

# VILLAGE LIGHTS
# GO ON

Despite continuing evidences of God's providential care and guidance, His work seemed to move forward slowly in our region. Many years of faithful service in the Vailala area of the Gulf District had produced little in the way of real results. Devilish heathenism, superstition, and fear were deeply entrenched in these western people for whom the Master had died.

I decided to make the matter of a real breakthrough the burden of my prayers, claiming the promise contained in James 1:5: "If any of you lack wisdom, let him ask of God ... and it shall be given him."

Over the next few weeks a plan formed in my mind that I feel was divinely inspired. I decided to launch out in aggressive evangelism. The problem was, How could I capture the people's interest? If I conducted a mission (series of meetings) in any one village, I could reach only a small part of the population. I asked my Master how to solve this problem, and a plan slowly took shape in my mind.

Deciding upon ten or twelve villages with an average of about fifty or sixty inhabitants each, I took my camera and snapped about two dozen color shots in each village, showing groups of old men sitting in counsel, groups of youth or children, mothers feeding their babies, or girls and boys playing by the seashore. I tried to take these pictures without the villagers knowing what I was doing.

While waiting the several weeks required for the transparencies to come back from Australia, I spent every spare minute preparing studies best suited to the Papuans. I whittled my studies down to about sixteen. I felt I could present these over three days, running five or six meetings a day.

My next move was to send for my fifteen outstation teachers, including some ordained men. In practically every case these men had worked for years without any tangible results.

Lining up this group of teachers each morning for eight or ten days, I handed each one typed copies of two sermons written in the Motuan language, beginning with the ones I planned to give when we launched into our evangelistic campaign. The notes on the subjects were very detailed. All illustrations and important points had been underlined in red for emphasis. I told them to study these notes carefully in the four hours during the morning while regular classes were being conducted and I was busy at the dispensary.

As soon as possible after school was over and the students had been given their work assignments, I called the teachers into the school and preached my two evangelistic sermons, having an interval between and at all times giving them opportunity to ask questions about any points that were not clear.

The next afternoon, the second day, before taking studies three and four, I picked out two of the teachers and asked them each to preach one sermon we had used the day before. I sat in the class and did not spare them in my constructive criticism concerning the weaknesses in their preaching.

The fact that the teachers were not told who would be called on to take the next two sermons under review motivated them to earnest preparation. They studied as they had never studied before. Our daily program became very interesting, for soon the time came when I sat down each afternoon and listened to preaching from my notes!

By the time the sixteen studies had been presented, my teachers were "rarin' to go." They were disappointed when I told them that they were going to listen to me preach again in a real campaign.

We arrived at our first coastal village late one afternoon, carrying with us sufficient food for three days, a battery (car type), projector and screen, and a pressure light. The battery was for operating the projector.

After dark we flashed our first picture on the screen. This was a picture taken in that particular village. The impact was fantastic. People literally poured out of their darkened houses to see themselves on the screen for the first time. After showing about half a dozen slides, I would announce that I had quite a lot more pictures to show them a little later, but first I wanted to talk to them for a little while in their own language. Then I launched into my first study, along the same lines as we would run a mission campaign in the homeland but much more simplified and suited to their environment.

From the first meeting it was evident that we had captured their interest, so we showed another half dozen slides and announced that there would be another meeting at six o'clock the next morning. They rolled out in full strength again. We had another meeting at 10:00 a.m., another at 2:00 p.m., another at 4:00 p.m., and another in the evening showing a few more slides. At the end of the three-day campaign, I made a call for those to come forward who wanted to join a baptismal class, and thirty-eight of the forty inhabitants joined. I left one of my teachers with them to carry the interest through to fruition.

We arrived at our next village, and prior to beginning our second campaign, I was confronted by several teachers, two of them ordained men, who asked whether one of them could

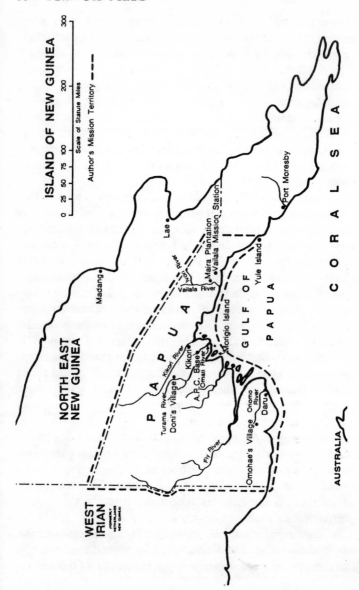

be the preacher for the next series. My answer was an emphatic, "No, you are going to listen to me preach again." This
was a larger village but produced about the same results
proportionately.

Then we moved on to Oveke's home village. At this
village two ordained men, Pastor Koivi (KOY-vee) and Pastor Paul Jama (JAH-ma), really pleaded with me to let either
one of them be the real evangelist.

I refused again, mainly because this was Oveke's village,
the very center of devilism and the home of the devil priest. I
feared that we might run into opposition seeing we were on
the devil's enchanted ground.

After the first evening meeting, I was confronted by one
of the devil priest's cohorts and told to get out of the village
"or else." Next morning during the six o'clock meeting I was
rather rudely interrupted and told that if I did not stop immediately, I would be dead by sunset the next day. The devil
priests like to get some part of their victim's person, such as
a tooth, a piece of fingernail, or even a hair of the victim's
head. This makes them sure of the death of their victim.
When I was told that I would be dead by sunset next day, I
ran my fingers through my hair pulling out several hairs and
handed them to the devil's ambassador as a means of ridding
myself of him.

During an afternoon meeting I noticed the devil priest
sitting some little distance from my audience apparently listening to every word being spoken. As I closed the meeting
the devil priest sent someone to ask how I was feeling. My
answer was, "Never better." He seemed amazed.

At all the meetings the next day the devil priest was
present. After every meeting he sent someone to ask me how
I was feeling, to which I always answered, "Never better."
That night at the closing meeting of the series, about fifty
people pledged to follow their Lord in response to my call to
join a baptismal class. Imagine my joy when I saw the devil

priest himself make his way down to where I was standing. He handed me a small woven bag that contained all his devil charms. The old fellow, in a breaking voice, asked how I was feeling. Again I answered, "Never better." Chokingly he said, "Master, I have tried everything I know of to puri puri you, but nothing has worked. The God you serve is stronger than the god I serve. I want to follow your God."

I should have burned those devilish charms that night, but weary after my third campaign, I left them until morning. Soon after I retired I was awakened from my sleep by a presence in the house in which I was sleeping. Then I felt hands stronger than mine closing around my throat—hands that were strangling me. In a desperate, choking voice I cried out, "I command you in the name of the Lord Jesus Christ to leave me alone!" Immediately I was released from the devil's power.

After a break of a few days, we launched our attack for Christ on the fourth village, but this time I gave Pastor Koivi the privilege of doing the preaching. Pastor Koivi's results compared favorably with the previous results. I told him that I would give him two teachers and that they were to conduct two series each in six villages.

Then it was Pastor Paul Jama's turn. I did the same with him but by this time we had no more teachers to do the follow-up work because we had six hundred in our baptismal classes.

Some few months later I felt sure we would baptize at least five hundred by the year end. It was with some fear and trepidation that I took my overdue furlough, for funds would not allow another European to take over my station and care for my interests. I was bitterly disappointed that I was not given the opportunity of cutting my furlough a little short so as to be back for the baptism. It was the largest up to that time in the Australasian Division in one day with 334 being baptized.

# THE BOAT WE COULDN'T GET HOME

On a number of occasions while in yearly and half yearly committee meetings at our Port Moresby headquarters, I had expressed a desire to have an additional boat for my work. The forty-footer I already had was a wonderful improvement over traveling by canoe, as I had done in the first years of my mission experience in the Vailala District.

The way had been hard at Vailala, because the only means of transport was by foot patrol for inland work or by canoe for coastal or river work. These treks used to take me away for up to eight weeks at a time. Often while traveling by canoe, I and my companions would be caught in a heavy tropical downpour that saturated our bedding. However, with only two seasons, hot and hotter, these drenchings did not cause undue worry.

Maybe it seemed like lack of appreciation to ask for a second boat. We had been thrilled when a secondhand forty-footer was purchased for the Vailala field. This meant that I could travel much faster, cover greater areas, and have extra time with my family. This boat proved a tremendous blessing, but it always worried me for it was deep drafted and was a potential danger in crossing river bars. It would not stand up if it happened to run aground in a running-out tide.

In committee a number of times I expressed my desire to have an additional small boat, shallow drafted, that could enter small waterways and thereby enable me to reach many more villages. Money was always needed elsewhere, and my small-boat project was given a low priority.

After some two years of bringing forward my request, I was truly grateful when from another of our mission stations close to Port Moresby, a so-called whaleboat fitted with a new inboard motor was voted to my field. It was just an open fourteen-foot boat, but it was ideal for my requirements.

The problem now was getting it to my field, for hauling it on the forty-footer would cause us to be too top-heavy for the rough seas that were running. The only alternative was to tow it behind the larger boat the 150 miles. I purchased three hundred feet of new three-inch rope for the purpose but had to wait several days because of angry seas.

On Thursday afternoon there seemed to be definite signs of a break in the weather, so I informed the crew that we would be on our way at dawn the next morning. We traveled all day in very heavy seas but had no difficulty in reaching Yule Island, the only real shelter on that coast line, just before sunset on Friday afternoon. Our plans were to spend a quiet Sabbath in protected waters, and at ten o'clock Saturday night sail for Vailala. That plan would give us ample time to reach the Vailala River mouth before the top of the high tide.

Late on Saturday afternoon a rather large coastal boat skippered by Captain Dave Lamont, probably the best skipper ever in those treacherous Papuan waters, dropped anchor close by. I inquired of Dave concerning the seas outside. He answered in one word—"shocking." He asked what time I was putting out and I told him 10:00 p.m. Dave replied, "You should be O.K., Elwyn. The seas have eased a little in the past couple of hours, and the weather report is encouraging. So by ten o'clock tonight you should be all right."

We closed the Sabbath, and during the remaining daylight made our way through a very difficult reef passage where one has to alter course every few minutes. We dropped anchor about 7:00 p.m. at a point from which I knew I could run out through the remainder of the reef on the compass, a straight course even though the passage was none too wide.

The night, which proved to be black as pitch, did not worry us too much as we would be running by compass all night. Shortly before 10:00 p.m. we weighed anchor and bore out into the night at full speed through the passage. We were no sooner clear of the reef than we found we were in shocking seas with no way back, for there were no beacons on the whole coast line except at Port Moresby.

I decided that the only thing to do was to go on, even though I could not see how the boat could weather the seas. I put straight out to sea for the first hour and a half almost at right angles to the coast line so as to be clear of reefs. It was almost impossible to maintain a course. The seas were crashing over the decks.

We had been running for about one hour when one of the crew members said, "Master, the whaleboat is gone." I couldn't believe it, but when we pulled in the new towline, we found it had broken like a piece of flax. It is extremely dangerous to turn around in heavy seas, but I felt I had to locate my "new" boat. With the aid of a powerful searchlight we sighted the whaleboat after about an hour's search. I knew it could not sink for it had large watertight tanks under the seats.

As we neared the whaleboat, one of my boys plunged over into that raging sea and was soon lost sight of. I shouted to the boy who was looking frantically for his mate with the searchlight to hold the light on the whaleboat and not take it off. Within a few minutes we saw a bobbing head come up near the whaleboat. As we watched we saw him climb onto the whaleboat. Somehow the boys got the rope to him. I

Again I turned our ship in the raging seas, and for about half an hour we searched for the whaleboat that the waves had captured.

couldn't leave the wheel to watch, but the others said that he crawled back along the rope to safety. Thus we had the whaleboat in tow again.

Not knowing where we were was disquieting, to say the least. We could have been ten miles up the coast or ten miles down the coast or, what was even more frightening, near the reef. We couldn't see a foot in front of us without the searchlight. I decided to put out to sea for another hour and a half.

We had been running the best part of an hour, the seas worsening every minute, when one of the boys shouted to me, "Master the whaleboat is gone," and sure enough, once again the three-inch rope had been broken like a thread of cotton by the mountainous seas.

Again I turned in the raging seas, and after about half an hour's search, with the aid of the searchlight, we found the whaleboat. I ordered my boys to run the anchor chain out. We had sixty fathoms (360 feet) of chain almost as thick as my little finger. Somewhat confidently I told the boys that no sea would break that. We again went through the same difficult and dangerous procedure as before, but at last we had the whaleboat in tow again. Now I was in a bigger turmoil than ever. Maybe by this time we were twenty miles up the coast or the same distance down the coast, or perhaps we were nearer the reef. Not knowing, I decided to put out to sea for another hour and a half.

We had been running only about half an hour when the boys shouted, "Master, the whaleboat is gone." I just couldn't believe it.

When the chain was pulled in, we found that the nose of the boat had been torn out and was still attached to the chain.

Turning in the sea for the third time, I decided that if we could find the whaleboat I would try to get the new engine out of it. It would mean undoing about a dozen bolts, tying a rope around the engine and hauling it on board. I asked my most capable boy, the one who had plunged into the sea on the two previous occasions, to take the wheel and try to hold the boat into the sea. I told the light boy to keep the light on the whaleboat and I would do the rest.

Picking up two crescent wrenches I was about to plunge into the sea when three of the crew clung to me and with tears running down their faces said, "Master, you can't go. If one of us is lost that doesn't matter, but if you are lost then we are all lost, for we don't know where we are." I knew they needed me, but I also knew that they would not know which bolts to undo. There was only one alternative — leave the whaleboat. It was already awash with water, with only the watertight tanks holding it in a half-submerged condition. This was an agonizing decision.

Although I felt that our boat couldn't possibly weather the seas much longer, I decided to put out to sea again. Not having the slightest clue where we were, I set a course that I believed would be straight out to sea. With the second in command at the wheel, I went down in my cabin and poured out my heart to the Master of the seas, telling Him that I knew He could rebuke the wind and the sea as He had when, with His disciples on the Sea of Galilee, He spoke those words, "Peace be still." I told Him that we were lost in heavy seas.

An impression swept over me to alter our course to the compass heading zero nine zero (due east). This seemed all wrong to me, but I hurried to the wheelhouse, set the course, and told the boy not to alter course unless I told him to do so. Then, going on deck, I posted a boy to watch for any sign of a village firelight. He replied, "Master, you would never see anything on a night like this." I asked him to listen for any sound of waves breaking on the reef. Again he replied, "You would never hear anything on a night this." The only way he was able to prevent his being washed overboard was to lash himself to the mast with what was left of the whaleboat's towline.

Returning to the wheel, I took over again, but every fifteen or twenty minutes I would have a boy take over for a few minutes while I went on deck to ask whether there was any sign of a fire or sound of the reef. Every time I was told the same words, "Master you couldn't see or hear anything on a night like this."

Some little time later I was suddenly impressed to make a major change in my course. This I did immediately. Again and again I went on deck to ask whether anything could be seen or heard above the crashing seas. At last the boy said, "Master, the seas seem to be calming a little," and then, in a matter of moments, we were in calm water. We throttled the engine right back and prayed. Shortly daylight broke, and can you believe it, we were safely inside the reef that we had gone out through at ten o'clock the night before. We were well inside the place where we had anchored.

We ran alongside Dave Lamont's boat and he called out, "Padre, I thought you were going at ten o'clock last night." I told him that I had, but he flatly refused to believe me. He said, "No man, regardless of what kind of skipper he is, could put out to sea at that time last night and find his way back in through the reef and be alongside my boat here before sunrise. Maybe a couple of hours after sunrise, yes."

I guess even today I would have a little difficulty in piloting a boat in through that reef in daylight, and in doing so I would have to alter my course twenty times, yet my Captain knows of a passage where our boat came in on just two compass headings.

Some days later when seas had calmed we made a thorough search of the coast line, inquiring at almost every village for any wreckage of the whaleboat, but it was never seen again.

# CONQUERING THE KUKUKUKUS

Two challenges that seemed insurmountable continually tugged at my heartstrings. One was the vast untapped Kukukuku (KOOK-uh-KOOK-uh) country and the other the cannibal region of Western Papua's hinterland.

The very name Kukukuku causes trembling lips among the Western Papuan tribesmen. Government patrol officers can testify that while on patrol they often have difficulty in retaining their hired carriers if they happen to see Kukukuku foot tracks.

These savage little people are the pygmies of New Guinea. As far as I was able to ascertain, they are not cannibals; rather they kill for the sake of killing. Murder seems to be woven into the very fabric of their superstitions and customs. A man has not proved himself unless he has taken a life, and of course, the more lives he has taken the better man he is. When a Kukukuku warrior presents his chief with a freshly killed human head from another language area, he is immediately given a hornbill's feather (rather a rare bird in New Guinea) to place in his fuzzy hair. I have seen many Kukukukus with so many feathers that their hair couldn't be seen.

The instinct to kill is so deeply imbedded in their way of life that their young women will have nothing to do with a young man who does not display hornbill feathers. The more feathers a young man wears, the more eligible he becomes.

These savage people are deadly with their bows and arrows. I wouldn't give them a shot at me at five hundred yards if I could avoid it. I have seen them draw an arrow and quickly fire at a little bird the size of a sparrow a hundred feet or more above. Inevitably, the little bird will fall to the ground and the arrow will most likely never be seen again.

One day while I was walking along a riverbank with a couple of Kukukuku warriors one of them quickly drew an arrow and shot, even though I saw nothing in the water at the time. Moments later a fish appeared on top of the water with half its innards torn out.

The Kukukukus use poisoned arrows against their enemies but never in their search for food. There are two ways at least by which they poison their arrows. One is by the combined sap of certain trees and vines; the other is by plunging the arrowhead in putrefying human flesh, which results in septicemia. Both methods cause violent death within a few days. Their arrowheads are often tipped with human bone or bone from the cassowary (a large bird related to the ostrich family), and are carved so as to have a barbed, hollow point. The poison is placed in the hollow and the bone is lightly glued to the arrow tip. The only way to get the arrow out is to push it through the victim. To try to withdraw it leaves the poisoned bone inside. Generally, a scratch from a poisoned arrow is all that is needed to cause death within a few days.

Strange and varied are the customs of the Kukukukus. If a mother dies in childbirth, which happens often, she is buried in a grave not more than twelve to fifteen inches deep with her face upward. The lower part of the body is covered, but the breasts and face are bare. From a tree high above a cord is tied. (The cord used is either a vine that entangles itself in the tropical undergrowth and stretches sometimes a hundred yards or more, or is made from the bark of certain trees or coconut fiber.) The lower end of the cord is tied around the newborn babe, and it is left suspended an inch or so above the dead mother's breasts. The theory is that if a boy child is destined to be a worthwhile child and to make a good warrior—or in the case of a baby girl, to become a good producer of children—then it would be strong enough to get to the milk supply. Needless to say, none survive. This places a stigma on the dead mother for being incapable of producing a worthwhile child.

Another custom peculiar to the Kukukukus concerns a man who dies or is killed. His wife or wives then become the property of the first man or men to claim them. The deceased man's children are allowed to live provided they do not ask for food. If they do, they are carried into the bush by the new father and their throats are slit with a bamboo knife. I have seen unfortunate little orphans crawling around on the ground searching for scraps of food. They crawl because they are too weak to stand.

On one occasion I found two of these little children who were skin and bones and suffering with large putrefying sores full of maggots. I took them back to our station where we nursed them back to health. Many months later I had to take my wife to Port Moresby for medical attention. We left the little Kukukukus in the care of Haru Hariva (HAH-rue hah-REE-vah), the head teacher, who was also in charge of the Vailala station. Haru later told me that from the time we left, the little fellows pined and fretted and could not be enticed to eat. When we returned a few weeks later we shed tears over two freshly covered mounds on the mission compound.

The Kukukukus are nomads who seldom establish a village. Instead, they live in makeshift huts comprised of a few sheets of bark leaning against trees or logs. They plant a garden and move on, knowing exactly when to return to reap their produce. Because of their constant fear of head-hunting raids from other language areas, the men keep awake all night to guard their settlement. They sleep during the day-light hours while the women plant the gardens.

Before my first visit among these people I prayed and thought much, asking the Master to prepare the way. The trip was carefully planned for the time when the fish were in the river's headwaters for the spawning season. The tribespeople can tell when the fish come in from the sea and travel up to the headwaters.

When the news spread around the campus that the boat would be leaving within a few days for the headwaters of the Vailala River at the fringes of the Kukukuku country, the crew came to me one by one with many and varied reasons why they would not be able to make this particular trip. One said, "Master, you know I am due for my holidays and I would like to take them now." Another decided that his wife's mother was sick and that he thought he should not be away.

I understood, for they had grown up fearful of the dreaded Kukukukus. However, I did not have any real difficulty in getting sufficient help to man the boat. I had with me my right-hand man, Pastor Paul Jama, a Solomon Islander, a man who had no fear in him.

After traveling up the Vailala some days, we entered a tributary, the Ivori (EVE-oh-ree) River. In a little while we knew we were in the Kukukuku country, because we could see the little people darting from tree to tree. Sometimes all that we could see was an arrow tip protruding from behind the trunk of a tree. Some miles up the Ivori we noticed a clearing where trees had very recently been felled. Such a clearing is a sure indication that a garden is being planted. They fell the heavy bush jungle and among the felled trees they plant their gardens. Gradually the bush dies down and their garden produce finds its way through.

I asked the men to drop anchor so we could go ashore. In unison they tried to assure me that they knew there were no Kukukukus here. Needless to say, they did not know because neither they nor I had been there before. My orders were to stop, drop anchor, and lower the dinghy.

Never before have I had such an energetic crew. They decided that they must stay on the boat to wash down the decks, polish up the engine, and in general have a spring cleaning. Pastor Paul and I rowed in the dinghy to the riverbank. He was a true soldier of the cross and was always ready for adventure.

I only knew one word of the Kukukuku language. The word was *miroki* (mih-RAW-kee), which means "come." Stepping from the dinghy and climbing up the riverbank, I called "miroki, miroki" until I was almost hoarse, but miroki they didn't. I began to wonder whether the boys were right in saying that there were no Kukukukus there.

Calling out "miroki" once more, we were surprised to see a young warrior walk out along a fallen tree that had come to rest some ten or twelve feet above the ground.

He had his arrow aimed directly at us. We were amazed when he answered in the Motuan language, "What do you want?"

"We are friends. We've come to heal your sick and show you a new way of life."

"You are not our friends. You are our enemies. You have come to arrest us for our killings."

It happened that some two years before, a government patrol had passed through a portion of the Kukukuku country and had actually walked in on a headhunting raid by the Kukukukus. The police arrested all the headhunters they could lay hands on and took them back to the government station on the coast and imprisoned them.

I had difficulty in convincing the young warrior that we were friends and that we had come to help them. But when I at last got it across to him, he called out "miroki" and his comrades came from everywhere.

How did this young man know the Motuan language?

Apparently, as a small boy he had been taken out to the coast where he had been sold for a large bush knife. The Kukukukus, being inland people, are hungry for steel and will sell a small child for an ax or a knife. This young man had grown up among Motuan-speaking people, but upon reaching manhood he had run away one night when he learned that some of his people had come down from the mountains to sell a girl for an ax. He rejoined his people and found his way back to their mountain retreat, but had to learn his own language again.

The young warrior became my able interpreter. Motuan was actually his mother tongue. Pastor Paul and I ministered to the people's many medical needs. While I treated some shocking cases of yaws and ulcers and extracted some teeth, Pastor Paul showed them pictures from an old picture roll. At last, when all their medical needs were met, we asked them to sit on the ground. I told as simply as I could the story of Calvary. While I was talking, Pastor Paul found pictures to illustrate the work of the Great Physician.

The old chief, a man covered with pig's grease, kept jumping to his feet and talking excitedly to his people. He would then sit down for a few minutes while my interpreter and I continued the story. Again and again we were interrupted by the chief. When I felt that we had preached more than they could possibly absorb, I told them that we would have to bid them farewell.

The old chief came over and hugged me until my white clothes were almost his color and told me that I would not be saying "farewell" because I was now their chief. This was the highest possible honor that they could bestow upon me.

Fearful of the consequences, I declined by saying that many days away my wife and children were waiting for the day when I would come home again. There seemed to be quite a bit of excitement, but I was absorbed in talking to the chief through my interpreter. The chief then impatiently took my arm and said "Take your pick of that lot." He had a line of women of all ages stretching almost down to the riverbank. Knowing that it would require great care to handle this situation, I told him that I would not know which one to choose. He replied, "It need not be one. You can have as many as you like." This was the second highest honor that they could bestow upon me.

I tried to explain that I could not be their chief and that I could not take any of their women for a wife. Immediately the air was tense with excitement—savage, writhing tribesmen tipping their arrows in their own blood, the last act before they take life. One has to think quickly or he may not have the chance to think again.

I spoke just one word and that was the name of Jesus, a name that they had never heard before that day. Immediately the warriors laid down their bows, arrows, and spears side by side on the ground, a sign among primitive people that they want to make peace. What power there is in that name—power that even you and I know little about!

The laying down of their weapons gave me an opportunity to explain my reasons for not becoming their chief and why I could not accept a wife from among their people. Finally, I promised that I would return. The old chief asked, "How do we know that your promise is true?"

I said, "My promise is true. I will return. I will come again."

"All right then, we will give you a gift."

Apparently this was their way of sealing a contract. I knew from past experience the time it can take native people to give a gift. It generally means a trek to their gardens to bring back pineapples, a bunch of bananas, or other garden produce. I was eager to get my boat into sheltered waters, because a storm was looming over the Owen Stanley Range.

I tried to explain that I would not be able to accept their gift but gave the promise again that I would return. The old chief shook his head and said, "If you will not take our gift, then you are a 'man belong gammon' (a man who is untruth-ful)."

Again the air was tense with excitement for I had added insult to insult by refusing the two highest honors they could bestow upon me and now had refused their gift. Again I saw spears and arrows being tipped with the Kukukuku's blood, and again I spoke the name of Jesus. Immediately they laid their weapons aside to make peace. I told them that I would take their gift, but I did urge them to be as quick as possible because the storm could burst any minute.

Pastor Paul and I returned to the boat but were somewhat concerned to hear a lot of wailing among the people we had left. Going back to the riverbank, I called out to my inter-preter that if their gift wasn't given willingly, then I would have nothing to do with it. His reply was, "It's all right, Master, we are bringing our gift now." You could never guess what the gift was—two little boys, one about seven and the other about nine years of age—the last two with royal blood flowing through their veins.

The old chief made a flowery speech; tears ran down his dirty old face. My interpreter told me that the chief was telling the boys that he was no longer their chief, that they were to render to me the same explicit obedience as they had to him.

I was perplexed because I could not speak their lan-guage, nor could they speak mine. However, I could not afford any further insults. Thus, I thanked the old chief pro-fusely and sailed away with my two little boys.

We had scarcely started downstream when the roar of the storm could be heard as torrents of water poured down onto mountains close by. This seemed to me to be an apt illustra-tion of the devil's wrath against us for having trespassed on his enchanted ground. We were barely out of the Ivori River when whole trees came washing down and out into the Vailala.

The crew adopted the little boys wholeheartedly, and in a

The two smallest of these five Kukukukus were the boys we brought to the mission station to treat for their large putrifying sores.

matter of days they had them talking reasonably well in the Motuan language. They would get a cup of water when they knew the little fellows were thirsty and offer it to them, saying "ranu" (the Motuan word for water). When the boys reached out to take the water, it would be withdrawn and the words "ranu, ranu" repeated. When the boys tried to say "ranu," the water was handed to them. The same thing was done with food, and within hours they knew how to ask for food or water.

The whole story was nothing short of an amazing answer to prayer. We had been led to perhaps the only man among the thousands of Kukukukus who could speak the language in which we worked.

Arriving at our mission station some days later, I announced to my wife and children that we had two additions to the family. After all, this was one way of evening the score a little with my wife because she had often greeted me with the same words when I had been away. The only difference was my children were a little older than the ones she had saved from death's door. The little Kukukukus—we called them Caleb and Joshua from the promised land—became an integral part of our household.

# 13 TURAMA CANNIBALS KEEP THEIR WORD

Haru Hariva was one of the most unforgettable characters I have ever met. As one of our earliest converts in Western Papua, he gave his young life to the Master and to His service. After a few years in our mission schools, he entered our old Miregeda Training School, near Port Moresby, where his brilliance and consecration soon carried him to the apex. To crown his success, he linked his life with a young woman named Kaura Muku (COW-rah MOO-koo). She was one of the most talented, consecrated, and outstanding Christian women I have known.

Haru gave his whole life to mission service. He proved to be an outstanding teacher in many of our schools, but his burden was always for evangelism. During the fifteen years that I was associated with this champion of the cross, I found him to be without parallel in opening up new work. Many times I have sailed away, leaving him behind among savage people. Cannibalism and headhunting vanished under the impact of Haru's preaching. Both he and I have known how hard it is to conduct a mission service in villages where we could breathe the pungent atmosphere of human flesh being cooked in the bamboo cooking tubes.

As a linguist, Haru had no rival. I was amazed to learn

that Haru spoke no less than thirty-two languages and dialects. I have never been in a village, coastal or inland, when I had Haru with me where I was not able to use him as my interpreter. He could always find someone who knew one of the many languages he spoke.

For years the Turama (two-RAH-mah) River region had been a special challenge to mission enterprise. Other mission bodies on a few occasions had explored the possibility of beginning work among the cannibals of the upper Turama River, but they had turned away. I knew that the gospel must go to these savage people and that the responsibility seemed to rest squarely on my shoulders for it was part of my large territory. (See map, p. 60.)

As I prayed about opening the Turama area, the text Isaiah 54:2 seemed to dominate my thinking: "Lengthen thy cords, and strengthen thy stakes." For some months I prayerfully worked out plans for an exploratory trip, which I felt would be the best way to evaluate the potential and the best means of launching an all-out offensive. Needless to say, I was conscious of the fact that it would require much more than human planning, for the enemy of souls would certainly resist any challenges to his domain.

To find time for such a trip seemed impossible. At last I managed to fit in nine days, the very minimum required. As the time approached my wife and I gave much time to prayer for the venture. We anticipated that the announcement of such a trip to the students would cause some real concern.

One morning, within three weeks of my planned departure time, I broke the news to the students at the close of our morning worship. It was as though a bomb had been dropped. In tears some of them pleaded with me not to go, for they felt it would be good-bye forever. When they became fully convinced that I was going, without even a suggestion by me or to me they decided to have prayer meeting every morning and every evening. They worked out the whole format themselves. First, they prayed that the Master would bring me and my passengers safely back to them; and second, that the Lord would send His angels to prepare the way. Do you know that every person on the mission attended those early morning and evening prayer meetings!

As we neared the time of sailing, my wife became apprehensive. She wasn't a good sailor but decided that she and the two younger children should accompany me on this trip, for she felt that if I were to be killed, then maybe it would be better for all of us to be lost together. (The older children were in one of our schools in Australia.)

We sailed one Sunday morning with several teachers, including Haru, plus the crew. Heavy seas were running, but that did not worry me unduly, for according to the law of averages, we should have been out of the southeast season (rough weather). We were able to travel for the first couple of days in inside waters, through the great Papuan Delta, a vast spider web of rivers. One can travel eighty or ninety miles and not be any more than a few miles from the sea yet in inside waters.

By Monday afternoon we had reached a point from which it was necessary to put out to sea for two or three hours to cross a bay before entering the mouth of the Turama River. To do this meant taking the sea beam on, but this was impossible because the waves had not abated. All we could do was wait for a break in the seas. Tuesday proved to be as rough, and Wednesday morning was even worse. However, the late afternoon showed definite signs of a drop in the wind and a running down of the sea. I alerted the crewmen that early the next morning, Thursday, we would make an attempt to cross over into the protected waters of the Turama. On Thursday morning the seas were still quite rough, but my precious time was running out so I decided to put out. We took a battering for a couple of hours, and it was a real relief to those unaccustomed to sailing when we entered the Turama's mouth.

The Turama is twenty-five miles wide at the mouth but is cone-shaped and soon narrows down considerably. It is known as the worst river on the Papuan coast for bores. A river bore is not the type of bore you obtain drinking water from or water for thirsty stock, nor is it in any way related to the pig family. It is a tidal wave with a high, abrupt front. The Turama River continually carries a tremendous volume of water that increases at the peak new- and full-moon tides. This flow forces back the incoming tides until they build a wall of water that eventually drives up the river, traveling as far as ninety or one hundred miles.

The water of the Turama may run downstream for nine hours and then run backwards or upstream for the next three hours. The rise or fall in the whole length of the river is minimal, because of the flat delta country. Big tides cause big bores, king-sized tides cause king-sized bores, which can mean a wall of water twelve feet high, followed a few yards behind by another, slightly smaller, and a third about the same distance behind the second.

Personally, I have never seen a bore more than about eight feet; but even a three- or four-foot bore is a frightening experience and can mean losing your boat if it should catch you beam on. A number of boats have been lost in the Turama's lower water because of bores.

All day we traveled up and up, until near sunset we were opposite a large village on the riverbank. About a quarter of a mile out from the village, we decided to drop anchor for the night. Because I had a new diesel engine in the boat and it was due for an oil change and service, I suggested that Pastor Koivi and two of the teachers might like to go over to the village with a picture roll. Perhaps they could conduct a meeting and tell the people as simply as possible the story of Christ who died for them. They agreed to go, for they had no idea how to service the boat engine.

They had been gone only a little over half an hour when

my wife told me that they were on their way back. As soon as I saw Koivi's face I knew something was wrong. "Master, we are wasting our time here. They are not the least bit interested." He told me that he had never seen the depths of heathenism he had seen that night. What he saw would not bear repeating here, but sodomy was rife.

I am sure that if I had seen what he saw I would have reacted much the same way. He and I agreed that the gospel certainly must go to these people, and it certainly would in God's way and time. Had we not been told that the gospel must go to every nation, and kindred, and tongue, and people, and that from these people the Master would gather some who would one day shine out in His wonderful kingdom?

Next morning at dawn we set out again, pushing up and against the fast-flowing waters. Toward midday we saw several canoe loads of nearly naked people coming downstream, waving energetically. Apparently they were trying to get us to stop. Even though my wife wanted me to stop, I decided that we would keep going.

As the canoes came closer, my wife said, "Please stop and see what these people want."

"I am not stopping."

As the canoes passed close by my wife said, "I do wish you had stopped. Those people were crying."

Again I answered, "I am not stopping. Those people have never seen this boat before. They would not know us." I was eager to reach a headwater village described by a government patrol officer before sunset.

Every few miles we passed villages until, near sunset, we dropped anchor at the village I had hoped to reach. For the opening Sabbath meeting we went ashore and gathered together a few people and told, as simply as possible, the grand old story. Even though they were few in number—only about fifteen—they sat spellbound as they listened to the "Big fella Masta on top, Masta bilong all."

At the close of this meeting they assured us that by morning they would have many more people waiting to hear us. During the night they went out in the bush to where many were living in temporary houses while planting new gardens. Also they gave the word to a village we had passed quite a distance back on the river only a short walking distance away.

Six o'clock the next morning we were thrilled to see forty or fifty adults eagerly waiting for us. After trying to teach them some simple choruses, I spoke for about an hour and a half. At the close, I said, "Now you can go and get some kai kai [food], and then when you hear the siren on the boat, you will know that it is time to come together for another meeting."

The leader of the group suggested that we go and have our meal but assured us that they would be there when we returned, for as they said, "We have never heard these stories before."

We immediately had a few more choruses, and I spoke for about another hour. Then I suggested that we have a break for breakfast. They said, "You go and have your break-fast. We will be here when you come back. We want to hear more of this wonderful story."

Turning to Haru, I said, "It's over to you, Haru." He then spoke for a good hour and at last suggested a break while we ate, but again there were the same demands for more of the wonderful story.

After a break of about two hours, at the sound of the siren, they hurriedly gathered together again, and Haru and I took meeting after meeting. Altogether that day we spoke for more than seven hours.

Unfortunately, I knew that early the next morning we had to be on our way back, for my tightly packed program would not permit any more time. We had lost so much time with the weather holdup. I felt that with a reasonable day's run, we should reach the river's mouth by sunset that day (Sunday).

I well remember that down in the cabin I poured out my heart to the Master, telling Him I couldn't understand why we were permitted such a short time, with all the waste of precious time caused by the weather and all the cost of fuel for only about eight or nine hours of preaching.

During the hours of the night as I prayed about this matter, a bright thought came to me. The next morning, taking Haru aside, I asked him how he would feel if I were to leave him, two other teachers, and two of the crew behind— five in all—if I could buy a canoe for them to use in working their way down the great waterway. Haru said he would be very happy and would count it as the greatest challenge and the toughest assignment I had ever given him. The others readily agreed to join Haru.

Going to the village early next morning, I asked whether I could buy a canoe. The village people asked what size. I replied, "About a five-man." They said, "You will not get one this side of the river's mouth; we have only one- or two-man canoes in this river." I felt that the risks would be too great with separate canoes, so decided I would have to abandon the idea, unless the next village had a large canoe.

We bade farewell and within an hour anchored at a rather large village on the western bank, where I asked whether I could buy a five-man canoe. The people there also assured me that I would not get one this side of the river's mouth. Because of the bores, they use only single- or two-man canoes that they can carry above water level when they hear a bore coming. A big bore can be heard for nearly an hour before it reaches you, like the sound of a coming tornado.

Returning to the boat, I asked the boys to wind up the anchor. I went to my cabin again and asked, "Master, why all this cost of time and fuel and so little accomplished?"

As I started the engine a man in a canoe pulled up alongside the boat and said, "I have a canoe I'll sell you."

"What size?"

"About a five-man."

Impatiently I said, "Why didn't you tell me that while I was over in your village?"

He said, "Master, it is not in the village, it is up above the village where you spent yesterday taking meetings."

Needless to say, I was concerned about the time we were losing, as we had already come downstream about an hour. It would mean two hours, at least, to go back against the strong current, but then maybe this was God's answer. I decided to go back.

Hurriedly we took this man and his little canoe on board and then traveled upstream past the village where we had spent the Sabbath. We continued on and on. Every mile I grew more impatient. Every little while I would ask where the canoe was. All I would get in reply was, "Master, he close up now."

About an hour above number one village, I said, "Listen, this is too silly for words. Have you a canoe or not?"

He assured me he had, and now said, "Master, now he close up too much." Shortly he asked us to pull over against the bank, and he led us about three hundred yards through heavy tropical bush undergrowth.

I am afraid my patience was about exhausted, for I couldn't see any reason why he would have a canoe so far from the river. "I'm going to have to go back and forget about the canoe."

"No, Master, him he stop." Just then he showed me the canoe. Do you know what it was? A tree that had recently been felled, with not even the top of the tree cut off. In making dugout canoes the men cut a log off to the desired length and then hollowed out the inside with an ax. Disgustedly, I walked back to the boat and produced a new shiny ax and a new eighteen-inch bush knife. Holding them up, I said, "They could have been yours for a five-man canoe."

The man pleaded with me to let him have the ax and knife. Money, of course, was unknown in this region. He promised that he would have the canoe finished within a week, a job that usually involved months of work. He said, "I will call all my people together; we will make big fires so we can work day and night till we get it finished."

I asked Haru what he thought. He replied, "Fair enough. You can leave me and the four you promised behind. We will wait until they finish the canoe."

I was almost fearful to leave Haru and company behind with a new ax and knife, for after all, the people were still cannibals and all they had to do after we had gone was to kill the five men, and the ax and knife would be theirs. Yet I knew under the impact of the Holy Spirit's power our preaching had made a tremendous impression upon their minds.

We took Haru and the other men, together with the village man, back to the village. I gave the boys sufficient food for several days, the wherewithal to trade for further food supplies if necessary, and a new file so Haru could sharpen their axes for them. I then gave Haru and his team explicit instructions that they were not to bypass one village as they worked their way down. They were to preach the gospel in every village. Whether they spent one day or one week in each was up to them, but I emphasized, "You must not bypass one village." We sailed away not knowing whether we would ever see them again.

This long delay had held us up till after midday, and by night fall we were opposite the same village where we had anchored the first night on the up trip, instead of being at the river's mouth as I had planned. This was the same village where Pastor Koivi claimed he had never seen such depths of heathenism in his life.

We decided we had no alternative but to anchor, for there were too many floating logs to travel by night. Almost as soon as we had dropped the anchor, I asked Koivi and some of the boat's crew to go over to the village and tell the people to gather together, that I was coming over to speak to them. As they left I expected that what I had asked them to do would take about twenty to thirty minutes. At the end of an hour there was no sign of my coworkers. After an hour and a half I became anxious. Finally, after about two hours I could hear the splash of the oars as the young men rowed back to the boat. Koivi's face was beaming and almost as round as a ball. I asked what had happened. Koivi said, "I am not going to tell you. I've brought some of the people over to tell you."

Just then I saw a dirty old man, covered with pig's grease, climbing over the side of the boat. I could see by his dignified bearing that he was a chief. With him was a native policeman.

As the policeman came on board he was pulling off his police uniform saying, "Master, I am finished with the police force, so you take these clothes. From now on I am going to go everywhere telling the same story as Koivi told us tonight."

Then the chief spoke; he had with him a little boy about twelve years of age, and he said, "Master, this boy is the last of the blood line (the only one with royal blood flowing through his veins). I want you to take him on your boat to your mission station. Fill him up with the story we have heard tonight. Then, when he is full up, bring him back to us and we will empty him out, then you take him back and fill him up again, and we will empty him out."

Just then another chief climbed over the side of the boat. Koivi said, "You just wait till you hear this man's story."

Some three weeks before, this man was awakened by a bright shining light in his village. The next morning he called his people together and told them that he was sure that some great light was going to come to them. Then he said a week or so later he saw the same light again, but this time it seemed to be lighting up the whole river and shining most brightly on his village. Again he called his people together and told them that soon some great light would come to them.

Just a few nights before our arrival he had seen the light again, but this time it seemed to be shining on the river's mouth. As he looked closely he saw a pure-white boat and on that boat was a white man and a white woman and two white children. As he continued to watch, the great light lit the way for the boat to travel up the river till it came to his village. He finished his story by saying, "That is why we tried to get you to stop as you were going up the river, and that is why we cried, for we thought the great light was going to pass us by."

We talked on into the night of the Master's love and of the day when He would come back again, and how the light of His coming would be brighter than the noonday sun.

Surely this was nothing short of a miracle, a direct answer to the prayers of the boys and girls back at our mission station, for it was just over three weeks previously that they had begun their early morning and evening prayer meetings.

Furthermore, it was all part of God's plan that we were delayed in getting the five-man canoe. Otherwise, we would have been at the river's mouth instead of at the village where we heard these wonderful stories of God's leading and of the sending of His angels to prepare the way.

By traveling on the open sea, we were able to get back to the station Monday evening, but because of our delay, I stayed only long enough to put my wife and children off, then put out to sea again for appointments all around the field.

# 14

# DONI AND THE BRIGHT, SHINING VISITOR

During the weeks that I visited the outstation teachers and attended the committee meeting in Port Moresby, I was continually praying for the five men I had left behind along the Turama River and particularly for Haru, because I knew he would be the one to make the decisions. Because of minor delays, it was ten weeks before I was able to get back to the mission station and my loved ones again.

When I had greeted my wife and family, I asked, "Have you heard anything of Haru and the others we left along the Turama?"

"Yes, they came back about three or four days ago. Haru has an amazing story to tell, but I won't spoil it."

I lost no time in finding Haru. I listened to a fantastic story, which was later confirmed by the person concerned. As I tell this story, no doubt you will find it hard to believe, but Pastor Herbert White of the Publishing Department of the General Conference can verify its accuracy, for I later took him into the area, and he, too, heard the story.

The Bible speaks of things happening that we would find hard to believe: "Behold ye among the heathen, and regard, and wonder marvelously: for I will work a work in your days, which ye will not believe, though it be told you." Habakkuk 1:5.

The upper Turama people, true to their promise, completed the canoe within a week. While they worked on the canoe, Hari and his team preached day by day to the people. As soon as the canoe was completed, Haru handed over the new ax, the knife, file for sharpening the axes, and some fishhooks thrown in for good measure. Then he and his companions began their long trip downstream, spending a day or so in each village, sometimes more. One day as they rounded a bend in the river they saw several small canoes half a mile or more ahead. Some of these canoes disappeared into the overhanging undergrowth on the riverbank. Reaching the spot, they found a small opening into another tributary called the Wamuri (wah-MOO-ree) River. However, by the time they had found the opening, the canoes were nowhere in sight.

All except Haru were in favor of going on, for there was no village in sight. However, Haru said, "Did not Pastor Martin tell us we were not to bypass one village? We must find where the canoe people came from." So they traveled up the small river several miles till at last they came to a village.

I should explain that the Turama villages were not villages in the true sense of the word, for there was only one house, call a *dubu*, which could be one or two hundred yards in length. One I saw was almost four hundred yards long. Inside lived men and women, boys and girls, pigs and dogs, and on the sides of dubu, about shoulder high, were racks and racks of human skulls, grim reminders of cannibalistic feasts.

On reaching the village, Haru's band was surprised to find that it appeared deserted. Soon, however, they found that the people were inside enjoying a feast of human flesh. As soon as it could be arranged, Haru gathered the people together in a little clearing where he produced a picture roll and began telling the story of the One who had changed him from a heathen to an ambassador of Jesus Christ.

Haru said that he had been speaking only about five minutes through an interpreter, when an old man, whom he recognized immediately as a chief, came in and sat among the listeners. Almost immediately the chief jumped to his feet and said, "Take notice of this, my people. It's true, it's true."

Haru continued his story only to be interrupted intermittently by the chief, saying, "It's true, it's true. Take notice of it, my people."

Haru was impatient and almost exasperated because of the frequent interruptions.

When the meeting concluded Haru walked over to the chief and said, "Have you heard this story before?"

The chief answered, "No, never, but I know it's true."

"Then somebody must have told you this story."

"No, never." The chief was positive, but he emphasized. "It's true, it's true, I know it's true."

Almost in desperation Haru said, "Listen, if you know it's true, then how do you know?"

"My name is Doni (Daw-nee). Some weeks ago I was asleep in this big dubu and was awakened to see a man clothed in garments so bright and shining that I could not look upon them. This man said, 'Doni, you are to leave your village and go back into the mountains and build yourself a house there. If you do so I will come again.' "

Doni was so impressed that early the next morning he called his people together and told them what he had seen and heard. He gave orders for the people to go back into the mountains and build him a house. The villagers had never heard of anything so ridiculous and thought he must have become mentally deranged, but they dared not disobey his commands, for when a village chief speaks, his people do not ask the reason why.

A few days later, when the house was completed, Doni was ready to take his wife and three children to the mountains. They objected strongly, but they, too, eventually obeyed.

The very first night that Doni and his family were in their new home the visitor came again, clothed in the same white, bright garments which Doni described as "brighter and much whiter than the noonday sun." The visitor said, "Doni, tomorrow you are to leave your house and return to your village. You are to destroy all your pigs and, if you do so, I will come again."

To carry out this command required more sacrifice—shall I say more faith—because his pigs were his wealth. Men bought their wives and their land with pigs and could even settle differences with their enemies by exchanging pigs, but, as he said, "More than anything in the world I wanted to see that visitor again."

Early the next morning Doni returned to his village and had all seventy of his pigs destroyed. His people, after this, thought that surely he was "long, long" (mad). For days they feasted on swines' flesh, but Doni refused to eat or touch any of it and would not allow his wife and children to eat it.

Back in his mountain home that night the visitor came again dressed in the same way. This time he said, "Doni, tomorrow you are to go out to your garden and bring in sufficient food, for the next day you are not to go to your garden, you are not to go fishing, or hunting in the bush, but remain in your house. If you do that I will come again."

That day at home was the most wonderful day he had ever spent, because he felt that he was in the presence of the visitor, even though he could not see him during the daylight.

In the darkness after that wonderful day, the visitor said, "Doni, tomorrow you are to go out to your garden and bring in produce sufficient for several days, place it outside your door, but do not use it. If you do that, I will come again."

Doni said that by this time he was prepared to do anything, for more than anything in the world he wanted to see the visitor again. He could hardly wait for the next visit. Yet he wondered why he should be told to bring the garden produce and not use it but leave it outside his door.

That night, when the produce was outside the door in several bundles called *billums* (woven string bags), the visitor came again and said, "Doni, tomorrow morning you are to go outside your house. There you will find a measure by which you are to measure your garden produce. If you do that, I will come again."

Sure enough, outside his house the next morning there was a measure, perhaps a little different from the types we are used to. It was in the form of a pole about four inches thick and about fourteen feet long. Doni began with his *kau kau* (sweet potatoes) and put the first one at the first mark. Then he noticed that there was another mark, so he put one at that, and another and another, up to five, six, seven, eight, and nine. Then another mark appeared right near the end of the pole. It was separated quite a distance from the other nine marks. So he put a kau kau on that mark too, and then he began from the beginning to do the same thing again. Not only did he measure out his kau kau like this but also his pineapples, pawpaws, bananas, and in fact, all his produce.

There he left it all not knowing the reason why.

That night the visitor came and said, "Doni, the food beside marks one, two, three, four, five, six, seven, eight, and nine is yours. Do what you like with it, but the food alongside mark ten is mine. It is to be put in a billum, but otherwise is not to be touched. If you do that, I will come again."

In the dead of night as Doni was waiting for his visitor to come, all of a sudden the whole area seemed to be lit up. Within moments the same bright shining visitor stood in his doorway. Doni said he always had to cover his eyes with his hands because of the dazzling brightness. This time the visitor said, "Doni, tomorrow afternoon you and your family are to gather up all your food, and mine too, and return to your village. When you arrive, my ambassador will be there. Give him the food that is mine, and listen very carefully to every word that he says because you will know it's true, it's true."

It was then that Doni handed Haru the billum of food. Doni, in telling Haru the story, said, "That's why I kept on telling my people, 'It's true, it's true.' I know it's true."

I set sail almost immediately for the Turama area with Haru and his wife and family. Haru wanted to return to be with "his people." I hadn't planned for this trip but felt that since I had heard Haru's story, it must take priority.

We found our way up the Turama and then up the Wamuri. The Wamuri was slow going for we had to cut away overhanging trees and limbs every few yards. Sometimes whole trees had fallen right across the stream. My worry was whether we would be able to turn the boat around when we got there, because although the river was deep, we had only a few feet to spare. Haru assured me that there was a place near the village where we would be able to turn around. Haru's word was sufficient assurance for me.

Haru Hariva, his wife Kaura, and their children in front of their house in the Turama River area, where unknown dangers lurked.

I shall never forget my first night at this village. I forbade Kaura, Haru's wife, and his children to step off the boat, for after all we were among cannibals. While conducting my first meeting that night, I found it difficult to tolerate the stench of human flesh being cooked in the bamboo cooking tubes. Stench is the only word I can use, because the victims had been killed several days before, and this was the last.

That night Doni himself told me of the bright visitor.

After two or three days with the Wamuri people, giving three or four meetings each day, I said to Haru, "How would you feel if I were to leave you to make this your base and to extend the work to other villages?"

Haru was jubilant. "I was hoping you would ask me to stay." I told him that my plan would be to sail for home the next morning and that I would be taking Kaura and the children with me, but that I would be back in six weeks. Then if he was sure that things were all right I would leave his wife and family with him.

Haru, great man that he was, said, "Master, I will do whatever you say, but I would like you to ask Kaura what she wants to do. I promise not to talk to her till after you have talked to her."

I went immediately to the boat to speak with Kaura. "I am leaving Haru here to begin work among these savage people. I am taking you and the children back with me, but in six weeks I will bring you back again." Kaura, one of God's great women said, "Master, if Haru stays, then I stay, too."

I sailed the next morning, leaving behind Haru and his wife and family. My work was pressing heavily upon me. I had seen my wife and family for less than two days in the past eleven or twelve weeks and knew that I could have only about three days at home before leaving on another patrol that would take me away for a month.

Six weeks later I was back in the Wamuri village and witnessed a marvelous transformation. They had built a new village. The old dubu was no longer used. Houses seemed to have sprung up everywhere and a church was being built. As I sailed up to the village I found a line of about two hundred people standing side by side, dressed in new *lap laps* (loin cloths). Haru said, "I want you to shake hands with my people." I shook hands, and shook hands, and shook hands. I asked Haru, "How come all these new lap laps?" He said that he had selected twenty young men and had sent them by canoe to the mouth of the Turama and up another river to where there was a plantation. There they worked as long as it took to earn ten or twelve lap laps each. They then returned quickly to precede my return. Haru had not only organized the building of a new village and the purchase of new lap laps for everyone, but he himself had visited people in all the nearby villages and as a result of his preaching they, too, were there to meet me.

As soon as I found a few minutes to spare, I spoke to Doni. "Your people should finish with their cannibalism," I said. "Master, we decided to end that the first night after you left. We have left that forever."

"Well," I said, "what about the village people. Isn't it time they finished with their pigs?"

Doni replied, "There are no pigs left in this village. We killed them all. We won't even trade with them again."

Doni asked me whether I would baptize him while I was there. I hesitated. I told him I would be back in another six weeks. If he wanted to be baptized then, I would be glad to.

I returned six weeks later—in fact, three days under the six weeks—but when I arrived Doni was dead. He had been buried a few days before I arrived. *Don't spare me, Lord, for not baptizing Doni. I should have known better when You had sent an angel from heaven to speak to him face to face.*

This experience illustrates how the prayers of the boys and girls back at the mission station were being answered. Because Doni first saw the heavenly visitor at the time the students began their prayer bands, I feel my confidence in prayer—in their prayers—is justified.

The whole story certainly put me on my knees. Doni was a man who, on his own admission, had never seen a white man before and had no contact with any mission bodies. Yet he received a lesson in health reform, kept his first seventh-day Sabbath, and learned about tithing before we arrived. Do you wonder that the Master has a thousand ways of finishing the work that we know nothing about?

Some years later when the work was well established in the Turama River area, all cannibalism was gone. Haru, too, sailed out into the sunset leaving many sad, lonely hearts and tear-drenched eyes behind. Why the Master permitted Doni and Haru to sleep I cannot quite understand. But the impact of His witness through them will never die.

Haru and Doni, without a doubt, were the two most unforgettable characters I have ever met, and I long with all my heart for the day when it will be my privilege to introduce you to Haru and Doni in God's wonderful kingdom where we will never part again.

# 15

# SHALLOW GRAVES AND BURNING TEARS

Could it be that missionaries on furlough from the South Sea Islands give the impression in their mission stories that all is smooth sailing and that skies are always blue?

Naturally, when we tell of God's work, we like to dwell on the highlights and tell of progress, but there are times when missionaries' eyes are filled with burning tears.

Those who have worked in difficult areas, especially opening up work among primitive people, face challenges and obstacles at every turn. They draw very close to the Master and He draws close to them. When the nearest human help is many hours—in some cases many days—away, one learns to lean heavily on the "everlasting arms."

It could be said that we "pray without ceasing." To pray without ceasing does not mean that we are continually on our knees, but it does mean being continually in conversation with our Lord. When the way is hard with a nameless dread and fear, one learns to spend more and more time in direct communication, in walking almost hand in hand with God.

Skies are not always blue, seas are not always smooth. Sometimes dark clouds block out the sunshine. Sometimes darkness deepens. Sometimes tear-dimmed eyes find it hard to see that behind the clouds the sun still shines. I want to tell you of one such dark and trying experience.

For a number of years the workers in Papua had felt the need of a more representative church building in Port Moresby. Eventually plans were completed and financing arranged for the building of a church near our Port Moresby headquarters on Ela Beach.

The mission committee selected me to take charge of the building program. My enthusiasm was less than complete because I felt that the load I was already carrying was too heavy. Some relief came when the leaders decided that all the outstation teachers should be brought in to the Bautama School for a refresher course. That meant not only the teachers from my field but also the teachers from the Central Papuan Mission and those from Pastor E. C. Lemke's far western field.

In order to begin the building project and gain as much time as possible, the committee decided that Pastor Lemke would pick up and bring in all my outstation teachers. This caused me some concern, for although he had been around the field with me on occasion there were many dangerous waters that he knew little or nothing about. However, it was a committee action, so I threw the whole of my weight into the building of the Port Moresby church. My team of Papuan men worked long hours, and the building soon began to take shape.

We had been working for about three hours on New Year's day, a Wednesday, when Pastor C. E. Mitchell, president of the Papuan Mission, which included my field, came hurrying to the building site with a pained expression on his face. "I have bad news for you. The *Lao-Heni* (Lau-HEN-ee, Pastor Lemke's boat) caught fire in the Turama River. He is still alive and also the baby, but it is feared that Mrs. Lemke and the two older boys are lost." He told me that the government was providing a mercy flight in a Catalina Flying Boat to pick up Pastor Lemke and the baby and that he had been invited to accompany the flight crew on the trip.

Later I was able to piece the story together. Pastor Lemke,

his wife, Del, and their three little boys had dropped anchor on Saturday night, just a short run from the village described by Pastor Koivi as the most heathen he had seen and where they had spent Sabbath. They had sent a number of the teachers ashore to sleep for the night, because there were too many people to sleep comfortably on the *Lao-Heni*. Soon after dawn, when the teachers had returned to the boat, Pastor Lemke, still in his night attire, stepped into the wheelhouse and pressed the starter button for the motor. The motor apparently backfired through the carburetor, and in moments the boat was on fire from end to end. Then there was a terrible explosion and most of the passengers were thrown to the water.

The mission had just recently purchased the *Lao-Heni*, a good boat. The only drawback was that it had a petrol motor. However, negotiations were under way to have a new diesel engine fitted as soon as we could purchase one. Apparently, when the anchor was dropped on Saturday night and the motor turned off, the carburetor flooded and benzine ran out of it all night. My guess is that the benzine spread all over the bilge water. When the carburetor backfired, the benzine on the bilge water caught fire from end to end of the ship in a flash.

Pastor Lemke dashed into the cabin and hurriedly got his wife and three children onto the back deck, where several boys were trying frantically to untie the dinghy and get it into the water. In haste they pushed the dinghy's end under the water and filled the dinghy. It was swept away and both oars were lost. Neither Mrs. Lemke nor the boys were able to swim. As the flames leaped around them they joined hands and jumped into the water. Needless to say, they were separated almost immediately by the flowing muddy waters.

One of the teachers, Ovuipi (ove-WEEP-ee), after seeing a baby's head (little Lester Lemke) bob up near him, was able to swim ashore with the baby. The teachers felt that all were lost except Baby Lester, for the boat burned to the waterline. After a conference in which they tried to work out what to do with the baby (he was only twenty-two months old), they decided to walk down along the river in case someone had made the shore. Almost a mile downriver they found Pastor Lemke, badly burned and dazed and unable to remember what had happened. He kept asking for his wife and the boys.

Some hours later as the reality of the terrible story unfolded to Pastor Lemke, he asked how they could get help for the baby. The teachers had already decided that the nearest European help would be almost two days away, so they set about getting whatever canoes they could and asked local people who knew the way to set off for an Australian Petroleum Company base in another delta river called the Omati (oh-MAH-tee).

By midday they were fairly well organized, but the village people refused to go for there was a bore due in about an hour. When the bore had passed they set out in the canoes with Pastor Lemke and the baby, traveling all that afternoon and night and the next day. At about two or three o'clock on Wednesday morning they arrived at the A.P.C. base.

After some difficulty they were able to awaken some of the white staff, who prepared bottles for the baby. I was told that the baby hadn't stopped screaming, for he hadn't had anything to eat for well over forty-eight hours. The A.P.C. staff did all they could for Pastor Lemke, providing food and treating his burns, but they realized that he was suffering more from shock than anything. As soon as the A.P.C. could get on the air the next morning, they radioed the story as best they knew it, and the government in Port Moresby in turn contacted us.

When Pastor Mitchell returned after the mercy flight, he told me that Ern was still far from well. He and the baby were admitted immediately to the European hospital at Port

Moresby. About an hour or so after admission, the hospital attendants rang and asked to speak to me. The head nurse told me that Ern was very distressed and kept asking for me. She asked me to keep myself available. He had been given heavy sedation, but she said if he didn't settle down soon, then they would like me to come. They rang about an hour later and said that he was asleep and probably wouldn't waken for at least twenty-four hours, for he had not slept for days.

Late that evening I suggested to Pastor Mitchell that he call an emergency committee meeting, for I thought we should send a boat through to the Turama area, since there could be a reasonable chance of finding the bodies of Del and the two boys. Some thought that the trip would be futile, not only because of fast-flowing waters but because of crocodiles. However, I held out that someone should go. At length it was decided that Pastor H. M. Pascoe and I should make the trip in the Diari (dee-AH-ree, "light").

Several hours of the next morning were spent loading sufficient fuel and food supplies. We took about six or eight sheets of flat iron, six feet by three feet, in case we had to make caskets. We also took soldering irons and spirits of salt (muriatic acid) for soldering. When all was in readiness I rang the hospital, but found that Pastor Lemke was still not awake.

After a prayer season on the boat we sailed at midday, and until near nightfall we were able to travel in somewhat sheltered waters. Just after sunset we set out through the reef; soon darkness settled around us. When I went to set the course I found that there were no charts on the boat. It is an unwritten law that charts of the waters in which the ship operates must never be taken off the boat unless being replaced by new ones. The charts had been taken off by a new crewman. What could we do? There was a choppy sea running, it was pitch dark because of a heavy overcast, and there was no way back.

After some dead reckoning, I set a course that I felt would be toward the mouth of the Turama River. Pastor Pascoe felt that I had set the course miles too far south and that we would probably end up in the Fly River. Next morning there was no sign of land in sight and Pastor Pascoe asked me when I expected to sight land. I told him that I thought we should sight land shortly after midday. Midday came, but there was no sign of land.

One, two, three, and then four o'clock and still there was no sign of land. My mate again felt that we were too far south. Near sunset I was near the top of the mast straining my eyes for land, when at last I saw a little dot on the skyline that I believed could be Morigio (maw-RIG-ee-oh) Island in the mouth of the Turama. A slight alteration was made in our course as darkness settled down once more. We knew that if the land I had sighted was Morigio Island, within a couple of hours we would be in treacherous waters, so we prayed that the Master Pilot would show us the way.

During the next hour one of the most fantastic electric storms I have ever seen came up. Pastor Pascoe was standing by in case the engine needed to be cut back to half or slow speed. There was continual flashing of lightning, which verified that the island was Morigio, and we went right through those winding, treacherous waters with the motor running at full speed. Shortly after 9 p.m. we dropped anchor in a little inlet on the side of Morigio.

At the first sign of daybreak the next morning we were pushing our way up the Turama River. By midday we reached the village where the mishap had taken place. We were somewhat surprised to see a government boat standing by. As soon as we were able to talk to the patrol officer we learned that he had been commissioned by the government district commissioner at Kikori (kik-KAW-ree), approximately one hundred miles away, to go the Turama River and find the place where the tragedy had taken place and see whether any of the bodies had been found.

He informed us that he had the bodies of Mrs. Lemke and one of the boys but that the other had not been found. He asked me to come and identify the bodies. I did. This was one of the saddest things I have ever done. The body of Mrs. Lemke had been found and buried by the Papuans. The one little son was found some days later.

I asked to take charge of the bodies, but the patrol officer said he would have to obey orders, which were to return the bodies found to Kikori for burial. I suppose I could be accused of telling a lie, for I said, "Pastor Lemke's desire is that the bodies be taken to Port Moresby for burial." The patrol officer was understanding and said, "If that is the husband's wish, then I must hand them over to you." He agreed to tow the large canoe that carried the bodies behind his boat as we traveled downstream.

As soon as we had departed, Pastor Pascoe and I set to work to make the two caskets. Imagine our distress when we found that the spirits of salt had been broken down, making soldering extremely difficult. Toward sunset we were ready for the difficult, heartbreaking task of transferring the bodies from the canoe to the caskets. As soon as this task was completed and the government boat was ready to leave us, I asked the patrol officer to try upon his return to Kikori to get a message to our headquarters in Port Moresby stating that we were returning with the two caskets and that we would berth about 10:00 a.m. on Monday. The *Diari* was not radio-equipped. We finished soldering down the caskets just as the sun set. We hove to for about half an hour while we closed a Sabbath that can never be erased from my memory.

Immediately after the close of Sabbath and during the remaining light we put out to sea through the dangerous waters. Again I had to set the course without charts, but it was with much more confidence this time, for with a few variations for drift and currents, it simply meant a course almost opposite what we had followed coming. I shall never forget that Saturday night, for it was a beautiful moonlight night. The sea was like a millpond and the old *Diari* had never sung sweeter in her life. What a tragedy that we were on such a mission. According to my reckoning we should have picked up land by late afternoon, but to our surprise we sighted Cape Suckling at midday. It was unbelievable; we had made the best time ever. By sunset we were well inside the partially protected waters and by ten o'clock that night we dropped anchor in the Port Moresby harbor, twelve hours ahead of time.

Early the next morning we learned that the president, Pastor Mitchell, had received the radio message on Sunday and, acting on it, had made arrangements for the burial to take place at 2:00 p.m. I was somewhat distressed to learn that the day before, Sunday, they had flown Pastor Lemke and the baby to our sanitarium at Sydney because of his third-degree burns, which would require skin grafts. I was sorry that I had missed him, particularly when he had been asking for me to come.

That afternoon we tenderly laid to rest Del and little Adrian, aged 4. Del was one of God's sweetest girls, a loving mother, and a devoted, wonderful Christian. We buried them both in one grave, the dear little boy on top of his mother. The other little boy, David, aged 6 years, was never found.

When I compare the little that I have done for the Master, the sacrifices made by Ern and Del and those two little boys, then all I can do is bow my head, for there is no comparison. I thank the Master for what He said: "Every one that hath forsaken houses, or brethren, or sisters, or father, or mother, or wife, or children ... for my name's sake, shall receive an hundredfold, and shall inherit everlasting life." Matthew 19:29.

# 16

# A PROMISE IS
# A PROMISE

The sting of the morning tropical sun could scarcely yet be felt as I stepped ashore with two teachers at a small village in the headwaters of the Turama River. As was my usual approach, I first cared for several sick people and gave a number of injections. We then gathered the villagers around and began telling the story of the Great Physician who will one day soon open blind eyes, unstop deaf ears, make lame men leap as an hart, and unstop the tongue of the dumb. Isaiah 35:5, 6.

I hadn't been speaking long when I noticed that despite the people's interest, agitated warriors were feeling for their bows, arrows, and spears with their eyes not on me but on their chief. Their actions suggested that trouble was brewing. It could lead to bloodshed. Just then a chief with about twenty warriors armed to the teeth stepped onto the village compound. I knew at once that they were prepared for mischief.

Through two or three interpreters I was able to speak to the hostile chief and his warriors. It took only a few minutes to find out the cause of the trouble. Two months before, this visiting tribe had brought a little girl to the Turama headwaters village and had sold her for an ax, or at least the promise of an ax. Apparently several weeks had gone by and no payment had been made. Now it was a case of the ax or else.

I asked the hostile chief with his warriors to sit down while I talked to him. But he had no intention of sitting down till he got the ax. Finally I convinced him that if he and his warriors would sit down and listen to my story, I would give him a new ax that I had on the boat.

Thus, the Bible story I had been telling had to be retold and this was a rather slow process using four interpreters. I had been speaking only a few minutes when the visiting chief jumped to his feet and told me that neither he nor his people had ever heard this story, and asked whether I would come and tell his people. I agreed. As the story continued, the chief interrupted several times by again urging that I come and tell his people the same story. Each time I agreed that I would come someday when the opportunity arose.

By the time I had finished my meeting, the formerly hostile chief came over and hugged me with all his strength. You can imagine what my white clothes looked like from the pig grease that covered his body.

Then I asked the chief where his people lived, expecting that it would be perhaps three, four, or five hours away. The old chief waved his hands toward the mountains and, with his little stone ax, cut a notch in a log. "You start at daylight," he said, "and walk all day till the sun has set. That is that mark." He then cut another and spoke the same words, and proceeded to cut another.

I was beginning to wish that I had never made the promise that one day I would come and repeat the story to his people. The chief cut another notch and then another. After each notch he repeated the words about starting at daylight and walking till after the set of the sun. When he at last stopped cutting the notches, I counted them and found no fewer than ten. That meant ten days' hard walking.

No one should assume that it would be possible to walk there in ten days and out in ten days and fulfill my God-given task. One would need to spend several days among the chief's people, and then one has to make friends in every language area that he passes through. This is done by caring for the sick and those who need medical attention and telling the story of the Master's love. I estimated that it would take eight to ten weeks to make such a trip effectively. An additional burden after such a trip into primitive areas is that usually within weeks there are numbers of calls for teachers to come and locate in the villages visited.

I asked the old chief to give me some idea of how many people lived in his area. He told me that there were many thousands. Again I assured him that one day I would come. To break a promise like this one would lead to serious repercussions.

Days, weeks, and months slipped by and I found it impossible to fulfill the promise I had made. This worried me. The more I prayed about it, the greater became my awareness that a promise had been made and remained unfulfilled. My heart beat a little faster when I learned that the Taree (TAH-ree) Valley area had been opened up by the government, and the green light had been given for mission bodies to come in. It seemed to me that the Taree Valley might serve as a starting place to fulfill my promise to the old chief, because, by my reckoning, I could reach his area in two or three days' walking (about forty to sixty miles), whereas to go in from the head of the Turama River would have meant more than two hundred miles of travel.

Several times I unburdened my heart to the president of the Coral Sea Union. Several times I asked while in yearly and half-yearly committee meetings that we might do something about opening up the Taree Valley. Year after year lack of funds stymied such a venture, and to add to the burden the Lord had laid upon me, I heard that two other mission bodies had already become well established in the Taree Valley.

Imagine my joy when one day, while sitting in committee in Lae, New Guinea, headquarters of the Coral Sea Union Mission, I learned that funds had been made available to penetrate a little deeper in our gospel outreach. It took less time than it takes to say it to put me on my feet and ask that consideration now be given to opening up the Taree Valley.

After thorough discussion of the pros and cons, a motion was passed that Pastors F. T. Maberly, Lou Greive, and I make a trip into the Taree area, where an airstrip had been made, to investigate the possibility of purchasing land on which to establish a mission. Possibly the only reason I was asked to be one of the three to go was that I knew the Motuan language, which was the language used by government patrol officers and native police.

The three of us lost little time in chartering a light aircraft. We took with us a tent and sufficient bedding and clothes to last us a week, as well as the wherewithal to trade with the tribespeople.

The Taree Valley people, an interesting and colorful people, gave us quite a welcome, but we were disappointed to learn that government restrictions would keep us within a one-mile radius. And that in our search for suitable land to establish a mission, we would have to be accompanied by an armed local policeman.

The next day we began the difficult task of making friends with the Taree people and at the same time asking whether they would be prepared to sell us land. Actually we were not able to purchase any land outright, but when the owners of land who are willing to sell can be found, then the land is purchased by the government and leased at a nominal rent on a ninety-nine-year basis.

We felt that the Master was with us, because on the second day we found a suitable piece of land and the people were willing to let us have it. We arranged to meet the owners the next morning at the government station to complete the necessary documents. But when the time came, the government patrol officer informed us that the people did not wish to let us have the land. Of course this meant beginning all over again.

After searching another day and a half we were told of a people who wished to make ground available to us. Although it proved to be not quite as suitable, we decided we had better close the deal. Again arrangements were made to meet at the government office the following morning to sign on the dotted line, but alas, the owners refused to sign, saying that they had decided not to sell.

We began our search all over again and after two days' hard going came up with what appeared to be our next best situation. Yes, the people wanted us and were prepared to sell; so for the third time we planned to meet at the government office the following morning. You will understand that each offer to sell was made by different groups of people. We felt that we had come to the end of our tether when again we were told that the people had decided not to sell.

Soon after coming out of the government office, I spoke to the government interpreter, who spoke Motuan, and thus the Taree people were unable to understand our discussion. "Why is it that every time we find suitable land and the people are willing to sell, they change their minds when we get to the government office?" The interpreter told me that the government office had nothing whatsoever to do with their refusals. We were being followed at a distance every day, he said, by representatives of two other missions and when we found people who were willing to sell, they went to them at night and told the people that if they were to let our mission come into the Taree Valley, they would have to give up their multiple wives, smoking, betel nut chewing, and pigs.

It seemed that we would have to admit defeat. We spent another two days searching, but by this time the people showed little interest in wanting to show us land and no interest in

We had been turned down by many property owners, when early one morning this man came tapping at our tent with good news.

wanting to sell. We seemed to be faced with no alternative but to fly out again and wait until such time as the Master opened the way. As we discussed plans to charter the same aircraft to come in and fly us out, I began to feel more and more frustrated. How would I fulfill my promise to the old chief? We decided to spend much time in prayer that night, for surely if God wanted us to establish work here nothing could stand in the way. Only the angels of heaven recorded the anguish of our prayers as Pastors Maberly, Greive, and I poured out our hearts to the Master, whom we humbly challenged to do something so that our costly trip would not be in vain.

Toward daylight the next morning I heard someone tapping on the outside of the tent and stepped out to find a lone warrior who, surprisingly, spoke to me in Motuan. He told me that he and two brothers were going to offer us the very best ground in the area and that they would take us to see the land as soon as we wished. Then, if we were satisfied, they would sign it over to us the following morning at the government office. He also had something to say about not discussing whether we were pleased with the offer because he did not want anyone else to know that the ground was being offered to us.

I can still see him standing there in the early-morning light.

He returned some hours later with his two brothers and a local policeman. Our hearts were filled to overflowing, for within a short distance of the airstrip we saw the best ground that we had seen in the whole of our search. This was surely the answer to our prayers. The next day at the government office we lost little time in completing the necessary documents. All three owners placed their mark on the paper. The government officer stood aghast and said, "How did you get the best piece of ground in the valley?"

Today we have one of the most beautiful mission stations in the whole of our highland work in the Taree Valley, and have baptized scores of the Taree people.

Several years went by before I heard exactly how our prayers came to be answered so marvelously. While we were being frustrated day by day in our search for land with the constant refusals to sell, word of our arrival in the area reached the old chief, the one to whom I had given the promise that one day I would come and tell "the story." When told that Master Martin and two other white "masters" were in the area under his control trying to purchase land, and after he had established the fact that I was the one he had met at the Turama River, he sent three of his warriors with instructions to give us as much as we needed of the very best ground they had. Surely the Master works things out in His own ways.

# BIG SHAME: NO LAP LAP

As the impact of Haru's preaching spread from Doni's village area, mountain tribesmen came down in small groups to find out for themselves what had caused the Turama people to cease their relentless cannibalistic raids on the mountain villages.

For decades the mountain people had lived in fear. Their men dared not sleep at night for fear of an attack. With faltering and hesitating steps the heavily armed mountain people at last ventured into old Doni's village to ask the reason why the raids had ceased. Doni was now deceased, but they were told by Haru and some of the village people that they were no longer cannibals but were followers of the "Big fellow Master on top" (the Master of heaven). Unable to understand, the mountain people asked that they be told the story of the Big Master.

On one of my quarterly trips into the Turama River area, I was told that a number of mountain people representing several villages had carried down heavy loads of food from their inland homes and had sat on the riverbank for several weeks in the hope that I would come. I was sorry to learn that they had returned to the mountains the week before I arrived. They had waited day by day until, finally, their food supplies were exhausted.

On the Sabbath, during the Sabbath service, I asked the people of Doni's village whether they could remember the first night that I was among them and what they were doing. "Yes, we remember," they said. "We have a big shame (are very ashamed), for we were eating human flesh that very night." I then asked them to tell me why they no longer ate human flesh. Unhesitatingly they told of the change that had been wrought by the Master they now served and loved.

"Do you know," I asked, "that the same people against whom you used to launch your attacks are now waiting for the time when they too may hear of the wonderful Christ?"

In response, a young man by the name of Muto (MOO-taw) and his young wife stood to their feet. Then another young man named Kamoi (kah-MOY) and his wife stood, followed by another by the name of Kuruke (ku-ROO-kee), and yet another called Sapoi (sah-POY). These four young men and their wives told me that they would take the story to their former enemies.

I certainly did not expect this to happen, for they themselves were only twelve months removed from deepest heathenism. "I will not be able to pay you," I said.

"We do not want or expect any pay," they replied. "We can never forget the night old Doni, our chief, died. He called several of us young men to his side and said, 'We have a debt that we can never repay to the mountain villages for our killing. I am dying. You must take the story of the Master's love to the mountain people.' "

On Sunday morning I gave each young couple a lantern, two bottles of kerosene, an enamel basin, a boiler for cooking food, a lap lap for each man, and a skirt for each wife. They also received a large bush knife and an ax. Early the next morning after Haru and I had prayed earnestly for heaven's benediction and blessing to rest upon them, these four young couples gathered up their few earthly possessions and, after touching farewells and embraces, left for the mountains. My parting words to them were that I would visit them in the mountain villages in about six weeks.

On the patrol inland six weeks later I was accompanied by Alf Chapman, an Australian who was headmaster of the training school in my field. One hard day's walking brought us to a small village where we stayed overnight. After a few choruses and a story from the picture roll, we sat down with some of the older men from the village to learn of their customs and superstitions. Usually these old men are at first reluctant to talk, but I have always found that they can be encouraged to talk and often it is difficult to stop them.

The procedure I used was to pick out something that appealed to their ego. Perhaps I would say, "Is it true that you people are the fiercest fighters in the mountains?" or maybe, "Is it true that you are the greatest marksmen and make the best spears, bows, and arrows?" Generally that was all that was needed to start them. Then I merely interrupted them to direct their conversation along other channels, such as, "How do you bury your dead?" "How do you initiate your young men into manhood?" or "How do you determine when one of your girls has reached marriageable age?"

Two hours' walking the next morning brought us to the village where Kuruke had located. After greetings I asked, "How many people live in the village?"

"Forty-nine."

"How many are in your baptismal class?"

"Forty-nine, but there are a few children who are really too young to understand."

Amazing indeed after six weeks' work!

After spending a day and a night with Kuruke, we walked for another three and a half hours to reach Kamoi's village. Again I asked the same questions. "How many people in this village?"

"Thirty-eight."

"And how many in the baptismal class?"

"Thirty-eight."

We spent about the same amount of time with Kamoi, and then, after a further four-hour walk, we arrived at Muto's location. He had all 62 villagers attending worships and keeping Sabbath. Finally, a further two hours' walk brought us to Sapoi's village and again we listened to similar amazing results.

During the next eighteen months I visited these volunteer missionaries at about twelve- to fourteen-week intervals. I never ceased to wonder at the knowledge of these mountain people, displayed during their baptismal classes. I was amazed that these recently converted volunteer missionaries could impart so much knowledge.

On almost every visit inland I used to take kerosene and soap for the volunteers and from time to time a skirt for the wife and a lap lap for the husband, but otherwise they received no payment whatsoever. On one of these patrols I suggested a time, six weeks ahead, when all the baptismal candidates whom the missionaries considered ready should meet me at old Doni's village. Haru also had a number of candidates awaiting baptism in the beautiful river there.

When the appointed day came I was overwhelmed as I saw the number of people who had come down from the mountains to be baptized. I greeted everyone during the evening of the day prior to the baptism. Somehow I wasn't unduly concerned that I had not seen the volunteer missionaries. My guess was that they were busy visiting some of their own people in their home village.

The next morning when all the candidates were lined up on the riverbank and each name had been checked, I asked someone to find Kuruke, Kamoi, Muto, and Sapoi. I learned to my dismay that they had not come down from the mountains. How could that be? They had every right to be here with their candidates. Someone spoke up and said, "Master, altogether missionary got big shame too much because he not got lap lap." They were too ashamed to come down because their lap laps had worn out.

I could have wept for my carelessness and lack of thought. Here before me were the results of their work, yet they were not present to witness the baptism. If it had been reasonably possible I would have postponed the baptism, but I could not, as these lovely mountain people, with their radiant happiness and beaming faces, had walked many, many hours to demonstrate that they had been truly born again.

# THEN TO THE HIGHLANDS

During 1954 Mrs. Martin and I received a letter from the Coral Sea Union Mission headquarters advising that we were being transferred to Madang, on the northern coast of New Guinea, almost directly opposite our current location on the southwestern coast. This call caused us a good deal of anxiety, because the work in our field, particularly in the Turama and Fly River areas, was going like a prairie fire. This great field, consisting of the Gulf and Western divisions of Papua, had become part of our lives. I wrote to the Coral Sea Union committee requesting that they give further consideration to the call. I could not see light in moving because of the vast areas that were opening up.

To our disappointment the call was sustained, so we felt that we had no alternative but to pack up, for a call was a call to us, even though we could not always see the wisdom in it. The union mission committee requested that I take my mission boat to Port Moresby, fly from there to Lae, about two hundred miles away over the Owen Stanley Range, pick up another mission boat there, and sail it from Lae to Madang.

While in Madang I received a further call, this time to a place called Paglum near Mount Hagen in the Western Highlands of New Guinea, to take over a new mission station. The land had been purchased and a few temporary buildings had been erected. Within a few weeks my wife and children flew from Port Moresby to Mount Hagen to join me.

We were thrilled with the Paglum Mission station which looks out over the great Waghi Valley, a scene that continually delighted us. One thing that dampened our enthusiasm a little was that we had to live in a grass house with a bamboo floor. Every time there was heavy rain we had to put up umbrellas and place saucepans, buckets, and dishes in strategic places to keep our beds from getting wet. Besides, there were one or two holes in the floor and several more weak places.

My wife, who was not usually demanding, felt I should do something about putting a new grass roof on the house and repairing the floor. As far as the roof was concerned I figured that when it was raining it was too wet to do anything, and when the rain ceased there was no need. For some reason my wife could not see light in my calculations.

I wrote to the Union headquarters asking whether they could grant me sufficient money to build a new house. I received an N.S.F. telegram (not sufficient funds). It was then that I wrote at length explaining that we were getting wet each night now that the rainy season had set in. Within a short time I received a letter stating that the equivalent of $100 was being made available for a new grass roof and a new floor in the old house.

Almost as soon as I received this good news I took it upon myself to travel about twenty miles to where one of our church members, Frank Aveling, was operating his own sawmill. I asked, "How much lumber can you let me have for $100?"

"Enough to build the framework of a new house, provided you cut it yourself."

Being a sawmiller, I found this offer attractive. Frank let me have a couple of his trained men and all I had to do was to pay their wages, the royalty on the logs, and the cost of fuel for the motor.

The next few weeks were busy ones for me as I cut the timber, carted it in a trailer behind an old war-time jeep, and then erected the frame of our new house. When the frame was nearing completion, I again wrote to the union telling what I had done and asking for enough additional money to put a galvanized iron roof on the building. We found it hard to drink the water off a grass roof and were carting our drinking and washing water about one mile in four-gallon drums on the back of a small motorbike I had purchased. The water came from a beautiful clear stream.

Unfortunately for us the union committee did not take too kindly to my presumption in spending the money on an entirely new building when it had been given for repairing the old one. Furthermore, we were told that no more money could be made available to us. Undoubtedly I deserved the rebuke, for now we had a leaking roof, and the frame of a new building, and no money.

What could I do but pray that the money for a new roof would come from somewhere. Just two or three days later, I was on the Mount Hagen airstrip and noticed half a ton of galvanized, corrugated roofing iron for the Togoba Hansenide Colony. I notified Pastor Len Barnard, who was in charge of the Hansenide Colony, that his iron had been flown in. Len said, "It is definitely not mine, for I have not ordered any."

The name of the firm that had supplied the iron was on the crate so I wrote asking for some particulars. They answered by return mail that they had made a mistake and that the iron should have been flown to another of our Hansenide colonies—Hatzfeldt on the Madang coast. Further, they said that in view of the fact that it had already cost the firm sixty cents a pound to airfreight it to Mount Hagen, they would be better off to leave it there rather than have it airfreighted from Mount Hagen to Hatzfeldt. There would be no cost to

Our only disappointment in moving to Paglum was this grass house. The Union committee was a bit put out with what I did about it.

the mission, as the mistake was entirely their own, and the iron was mine. What a tremendous answer to our prayers!

Within a couple of days the iron was on our new house. We paid villagers to make bamboo plaits for the exterior walls and my wife and I, from our meager savings, were able to pay for a floor from Brother Aveling's sawmill. The Paglum Mission house cost the union $100. It is still the European mission house today but now has fibro sheet walls and proper walling inside.

We were surprised at the amount of medical work to be done at Paglum because there was a well-established and well-equipped government hospital at Mount Hagen. One morning a group of men came to the dispensary and when I asked the first one what the trouble was, he said, "Master, teeth he got pain."

I found that several back teeth were badly decayed. I proceeded to load the syringe to give an anesthetic before the extraction. As soon as he saw the syringe in my hand he ran for the bush followed by his friend. I sent a boy to tell them to come back. The patient returned to within about fifteen or twenty yards and shouted, "Master, you rouse him straight, no got shoot." He meant that he wanted me to pull the offending teeth without an anesthetic. He told me that he could have had the teeth extracted at the government hospital at Mount Hagen if he had wanted anything injected to deaden the pain. He said they had walked the ten miles from Mount Hagen to my station because they had heard that I pulled teeth without any anesthetic.

I tried to explain that the pain would be too much, but he replied, "Master, you try him tas all" (You try, that's all). So you know, I pulled four double teeth, and he never batted an eyelid. Then several more of the group asked me to pull their teeth but added, "Master, rouse him straight tas all, no got shoot." From then on I used to have teeth to extract every week. Men used to walk right past the government hospital and on another ten miles to get me to pull their teeth, always demanding that I "rouse him straight."

The Highland people as a whole have wonderful teeth. Almost without exception the teeth I extracted were from men who have been flown out to coastal copra plantations on two-year labor contracts. On the plantations they receive food rations of white flour, white sugar, and white rice.

We had built up a reputation not only for pulling teeth but also for delivering several babies without any real problems. The infant mortality was shocking in the area because of unhygienic conditions. One night as I was packing up my camp equipment for a mountain patrol that would take me away for several weeks, there was a knock at the door. Our nurse girl came to advise us that two of the women on the mission station who were pregnant were in labor. I wondered why they couldn't have picked a more convenient time. I told the girl to go back and get everything ready. I would be down in a few minutes.

My wife, realizing that I wanted to leave at dawn the next morning on my patrol, said she would go down, for probably they would be hours yet. Our second daughter, ten-year-old Edna—I always called her Midge because she was the smallest of our four children—said, "Don't you worry, Daddy, I'll go and help Mum."

I said, "All right. Off you go."

About two hours later, when I had my camp gear pretty well organized, I went down to see how the women in labor were doing. Calling at the first house, where I knew one of the women would be, I met Midge coming out the door. I asked how things were going, and she replied, "It's all over, Dad." I asked where Mum was and she said that Mum had told her to stay with this woman for she would be some hours yet, while she went on to another house. If the second woman was more advanced, she would attend to her first and then come back and help Midge.

I asked Midge whether she had tied off the cord all right and was she sure there was no bleeding. I asked several questions concerning the delivery, including whether the woman had hemorrhaged at all. Midge told me she had, but that she had given an injection to arrest that. I told Midge that I thought I should just check everything over to make sure that the woman was all right. She was indignant with me. I never had to do a thing.

Even though Midge was only ten years of age, she had seen her mother and me perform plenty of deliveries, but this was the first she had managed entirely on her own. Midge and I then went on to the next house and were in time to help deliver the next baby. Mum was a little out in her reckoning when she felt her woman would deliver before Midge's.

At the breakfast table one morning, I was giving the children a lecture about giving a buttock intramuscular injection, explaining how to give such an injection without danger of hitting the sciatic nerve. A young man had just been carried in, paralyzed in the legs. I knew that someone on a patrol had not exercised enough care and had hit the sciatic nerve.

Later on that same morning I was at the dispensary giving a buttock injection, when my youngest son, Llewellyn, came over. He was about five years of age, and as he watched me giving the injection he said, "Dad, I suppose you have to be a bit careful you don't hit his brain." He thought that paralysis was directly related to the brain. Maybe at that stage he wasn't quite as advanced in his medical work as his sister Midge.

# 19

# "PULL YOUR SOCKS UP, ELWYN"

With the annual camp meeting at Wabag coming up I sent a radio message to Captain W. E. Passlow, at Madang, asking whether he would be able to provide a charter flight from Togoba (near Mount Hagen) to Wabag in the Western Highlands. Bill Passlow, a most capable pilot and a wonderfully obliging friend, was the owner and pilot of Passlow Airways. My hope was to charter his Dragon aircraft to take Pastors Campbell, Greive, Gander, and me to Wabag.

Word came by radio that the Dragon would be at Togoba at 9:30 a.m. on August 2 and would lift off a load of 1,200 pounds. On the morning of August 2, I had our load carefully weighed at 1,000 pounds, consisting of personnel, luggage, and camp equipment. I had allowed two hundred pounds for Pastor Alex Campbell, who had not yet arrived.

The Dragon touched down shortly after nine-thirty, bringing in a load of urgently needed mission supplies. The supplies were unloaded and the luggage and camp equipment loaded, but still there was no sign of Pastor Campbell, who was to have come through by road from Garoga in the Eastern Highlands.

Captain Passlow checked the weights of personnel and cargo and then suggested that he would be unable to wait more than another half hour because he had another charter flight to do that afternoon. As we waited he commented that the wind was a little against us, so I immediately suggested that we would not wait further for Pastor Campbell. We would then be two hundred pounds lighter than we were allowed.

Bill replied, "Shove on the full load, Elwyn. She'll eat 1,200 pounds off here." I had already brought two other cases of supplies just in case Pastor Campbell did not arrive in time, so we loaded these two wooden boxes, bringing our load to fourteen pounds short of the 1,200. Just before we boarded the plane, I again spoke to the pilot, stating that the two extra cases were not urgently needed and that perhaps it would be wise to unload them. He replied, "She's O.K., Elwyn."

For the only time I could remember the wind was blowing opposite the way it usually blew. The Togoba airstrip has plenty of length but has a slight rise one way. This particular morning we would have to do an uphill take-off to take off into the wind. We taxied the full length of the runway. The pilot did the usual pretake-off checkup, which requires bringing the motors up to about 1,000 r.p.m. while the magnetos on each motor are tested separately for r.p.m. drop. At that moment I noticed that the wind had changed. I am a pilot so immediately started to undo my seat belt in order to walk up to the pilot and inform him of the wind change in case he had not noticed it. One of my friends, noticing what I as planning to do, said, "Sit down, Martin. Bill knows more about flying than you are ever likely to know." That was true and by this time we were beginning our take-off roll.

By the time we reached the end of the airstrip we were airborne but almost as soon as we were over the end of the strip we ran into a down draft.

All on board the aircraft, as well as the European staff at the Togoba Hansenide Colony from which we had taken off, realized that the odds were against us. What actually happened, I believe, was that we did a downwind uphill take-off. True, we were airborne, but we did not have sufficient air speed to cope with the down draft and within minutes were flying in a gorge at a lower altitude than the airstrip. I poured out my heart to God for help.

Nurse June Bartlett later told me that almost as soon as the plane was heard taking-off, she felt we were in danger and so petitioned our heavenly Father on our behalf. Beryl Doble, who was ironing at that moment, was overwhelmingly urged by a voice that seemed to say, "Pray, pray, pray." She dropped to her knees immediately and pleaded for our protection.

The text that seemed to occupy all our minds was "Call upon me in the day of trouble." Surely this was a day of trouble for us. All who know the highlands around Togoba and Mount Hagen know how rugged the country is.

Within a matter of moments after take-off trees appeared to be streaming by the plane's windows and then the wing tips could be seen clipping off small twigs and branches. With motors screaming, Bill fought desperately to regain altitude. We were flying in a gorge with towering mountains on each side, with wing tips being lifted by the skillful pilot so as to avoid hitting limbs of trees and grassy ridges. With perspiration dripping from his face, even though it was a cold highland morning, the captain said, "Hold hard, gentlemen. We are not going to make it."

Directly ahead loomed the towering mountainside into which it seemed certain we must crash, but just then our pilot cut both motors and deliberately banked steeply into a tree. Those words, "Hold hard, gentlemen," were the last words Bill ever spoke. He gave his life for us, for he must have known that he had no chance of survival in the nose of the plane.

All I can remember of the actual crash is the wing and fuselage fabric being torn away. Then apparently all were temporarily knocked unconscious, except the pilot who was killed instantly.

Pastor Greive was the first to regain consciousness. Gallantly, and in spite of his injuries, he pulled Pastor Gander and me out of the wreckage. He admitted that he was spurred on by seeing fuel pouring out on the hot motor. The wreckage never caught fire.

Pastor Greive immediately set out for help. Dr. Yeatts, his wife, nurse Florence Burdett, Mr. Bartlett, Mr. Doble, Mr. Cornell, the national staff, and some patients hurriedly set out for the gorge in which they believed the Dragon had crashed. They had heard the motors cut out and loud yelling of natives on the mountainside. Within a short time they were at the scene of the crash.

Dr. Yeatts found that the pilot's face had been crushed beyond recognition. Pastors Greive and Gander were battered, and I was more seriously injured. Preparations were hurriedly made to carry us out. Europeans and nationals did a wonderful job in making improvised stretchers and carrying us out of the rugged gorge. When I later saw the site of the plane crash and the gorge out of which they carried us, I felt ashamed for apparently I had rebuked them several times as they tried to carry me up the steep mountainside. The doctor, sisters, and carriers told me afterward that I kept saying, "Easy, easy, boys," and then apparently I would complain every time they got my feet higher than my head. I can't remember anything about the conversation or the carry in.

The Mount Hagen government doctor was rushed to Togoba, while a DC-3 with a doctor, Department of Civil Aviation officials, and emergency equipment flew in from Madang. It arrived shortly after we were carried to the Togoba Hospital. Apparently the control tower at Madang or Lae had heard Bill's distress call before the plane crashed. Shortly after, a fourth doctor arrived from the Bayer River Baptist mission.

Shortly after take-off, the pilot called out, "Hold hard, gentlemen." We crashed into a rugged gorge, but some of us survived.

Nurse Bartlett said to one of the government doctors, "Doctor, see what you can do for poor old Elwyn."

After feeling my pulse, he said, " 'Poor old Elwyn', as you call him, is in the hands of the Almighty." I heard him say that, but apparently he could not detect my pulse and my head was covered with part of a blood-soaked blanket.

Then Miss Burdett called a doctor over and said, "Please, doctor, see whether anything can be done for Elwyn." He too apparently failed to pick up my pulse for I heard him say, "I am afraid it is too late. He has had his choof." By this time I was prepared to call it quits.

The doctors in consultation decided to fly Pastors Gander and Greive to the Madang District hospital where their fractures could be attended to, but it was thought too late for me because my condition was too critical for such a trip.

I can clearly recall Dr. Yeatts coming over to me. Apparently a few minutes after the decision was made to fly the other two men out, he pulled the blood-soaked blanket back off my face and said, "Well, Elwyn, old man, how are you?"

"Doctor, I have had it."

Dr. Yeatts, with his stethoscope on me, said, "Pull your socks up. You're all right."

I certainly did not know what to believe, for one doctor had said I was in the hands of the Almighty and another that I had had my choof. Now here was Dr. Yeatts telling me to pull my socks up and that I was all right.

Long days and weary nights were made easier by loving hands. Everything possible was done to ease my pain and bring relief and comfort.

My wife, who had been hurried to my bedside in the home of Dr. and Mrs. Yeatts, was with me continually. She says that during those critical days I only had to move at night and Dr. Yeatts was out of bed and by my side feeling my pulse and running the stethoscope over my chest.

One morning I awakened with the pain gone. When the doctor came in and asked how I was feeling, I replied, "I am feeling like a round or two."

He gave me a once-over then hugged me and said, "You are coming through, you are coming through."

Indignantly I asked what he meant by "coming through."

"For several days your life has been swinging in the balance, Elwyn. I never thought you had a chance."

I immediately launched a counterattack by saying, "Roy, I ought to get out of bed and tap you on the beak, for when I was ready and wanted to die you said, 'Pull your socks up. You are all right.' "

With tears running down his face, he said, "Elwyn, I

never thought you had a chance, but I knew that if you for a moment dropped your bundle, that was it. This is not my work that has brought you through but the work of the Great Physician."

About two days later Dr. Yeatts decided that I had improved sufficiently to travel by road to Mount Hagen hospital for X-rays. The X-rays revealed severe skull fractures. The three doctors who examined the plates were amazed that one could live with such extensive fractures, and those who saw the twisted wreckage of the plane were even more amazed. No doubt because of the prayers of our wonderful Christian family our lives were spared. There is not the slightest doubt in my mind that I am now living on borrowed time.

# BIRTHDAY PARTY AT SEA

During our last term in the islands—spent back on the coast—I took my boat to Port Moresby for its annual survey. These annual surveys generally took two or three weeks to complete but sometimes more, depending on the amount of work required. The boat and its equipment were thoroughly checked and any repairs, overhauls, or replacements were made. The boat always had to be slipped so that stern bearings, propeller, and propeller shaft, also copper sheeting, could be examined and attended to.

When the boat and its equipment, which of course included dinghies and lifesaving equipment, had been put in order, an inspector examined it before issuing a certificate of seaworthiness. My boat had been on the slip for a week and a half when I was summoned to the telephone to take an urgent call from the Port Moresby Native Hospital. As I hurried to the telephone I couldn't even begin to imagine the reason for the call.

A doctor informed me that he had a patient by the name of Omohae (oh-MAW-hie), who was a missionary teacher in my field. He was extremely distressed and kept asking for me. I promised the doctor that I would get to the hospital as soon as possible. However, I couldn't figure out how Omohae could be there because I had only recently located him in a village in the headwaters of the Oriomo (ORE-ee-OH-maw) River some three to four hundred miles west of Port Moresby.

Within an hour of receiving the call I was ushered into a large ward of the hospital. There was the missionary teacher Pastor Omohae, in rather poor shape and certainly distressed. A doctor who noticed me talking to Omohae asked whether I happened to be Pastor Martin. Assuring him that I was, he asked me to try to find out why the patient was so distressed. He had been unable to find the reason.

As I sat by Omohae's bedside and talked to him in Motuan he told me the story. One Friday he had climbed a breadfruit tree to get fruit in preparation for the Sabbath. One of the large limbs snapped suddenly, and he fell heavily to the ground, breaking one leg in three places and the other leg in two places. Apparently the bones were protruding in three places.

It took the local people two and a half days by canoe to get him to Daru, the government headquarters for the Western Division of Papua. By this time his legs were terribly swollen and, to make matters worse, were fly blown (covered with maggots). The Daru doctor took one look at him and ordered that he immediately be given antitetanus injections and flown to Port Moresby as a stretcher case.

Almost as soon as Omohae arrived at the Port Moresby hospital, he was taken into the operating theater where some hours were spent attending to his shocking injuries. When I saw him both his legs were in casts from his thighs to his toes. He told me that he was deeply concerned for his wife and several small children. They could not speak the language in the new area, and he was afraid that they might be short of food. Then he added that his wife was expecting a baby in six to eight weeks.

I promised Pastor Omohae that as soon as possible after my boat came off the slip the next day, I would get through to the Oriomo River to pick up his wife and family. That promise seemed to make all the difference to the patient.

This emergency interrupted my schedule, for I had not planned to go to the far end of my field for several weeks until it was time to pick up the students from that section for the new school year. However, there were several matters in that part of the field that needed attention so I conferred by telephone with Pastor J. B. Keith, the president of the Coral Sea Union Mission in Lae, New Guinea. Arrangements were made for Pastor Keith to meet me at Daru four days later. I then sent a radio message to A. G. Chapman, the teacher in charge of the training school in my field, asking him to meet me at my headquarters in about thirty-six hours and to be ready to sail with me for the other end of the field to pick up the students. Brother Chapman lived about four to five miles from my station.

We had a rather lively ride from Port Moresby to the mouth of the Vailala River, for the seas were anything but calm. Within an hour of crossing the Vailala bar we dropped anchor at my headquarters and I was happy to find Brother Chapman waiting for me. Jokingly I assured him that he would be in for a long ride for the seas were very rough.

The next morning we put out to sea again and took a battering for the next twenty hours, for we had a beam sea that caused the boat to roll excessively. It was certainly good to come into the partially protected waters of Daru Island. Pastor Keith was waiting there for us. After spending several hours attending to mission business at the government headquarters, we sailed for the Oriomo River. It is always a treat to get into inside river waters after having days at sea in rough weather.

We found that Mrs. Omohae and the children were well, but I was concerned to find that the baby would be due much sooner than her husband had given me to understand.

"I am sorry, indeed," I told her, "but I couldn't possibly

think of taking you back to your home village now, for the seas are heavy. To take you out into seas like that would bring on labor right away."

She pleaded with me to take her and the children with us on the boat. She was worried because of the language problem and so tried to convince me that she had five or six weeks to go. I argued, "You most certainly have not. You could not possibly go five or six weeks. My guess would be five or six days."

Upon seeing how emotionally upset she became, I examined her and told her that the baby could be born at any time, but because of her mental distress I would take her. She was most grateful and thanked me profusely. She insisted that I would soon learn that she was right and that I was wrong, for she claimed she had kept a careful record of her time.

I knew I was going against my better judgment, but in view of my promise to her husband and because she was so emotionally upset when she thought I would leave her behind, I had to take her. I reasoned it would be extremely difficult for her when the time for delivery came to be among people whom she could not understand.

Some hours later when we headed out of the mouth of the Oriomo River, we found that the heavy seas had not abated in any way. The next two hours we ran in reasonably sheltered waters and then entered into the rough seas. I was at the helm for the next few hours as we passed through difficult and dangerous waters, which were made many times more difficult because of the mountainous seas. The students we had picked up at Daru and in the Oriomo area were all seasick.

About halfway through the treacherous waters, one of the crew came hurrying to the wheelhouse and excitedly said, "Master, this fella meri close up too mus he catchim picanin. Please you come quik time." He was telling me that the woman was in labor and that I should come quickly. Turning to my second-in-command I asked whether he could take command of the ship through the remainder of the difficult waters. He replied, "Master, me no enough, me no savy this fellow passage suppose he got lik lik sea me enough along try him thats all." (He could not do it; he did not know the passage through these dangerous waters. If there were no heavy seas he would be prepared to try, but not now with these seas.)

I told the crewmen that it was virtually impossible for me to leave the wheel, for no one else knew the passage, so I suggested that he ask Pastor Keith or Mr. Chapman to deliver the baby.

Pastor Keith and Mr. Chapman immediately came to the wheel, and throwing their hands up in horror, declared that they wouldn't even have a clue about how to proceed. They had never delivered a baby in their lives.

Within a very short time the lad was back again urging me to come, "Picanin he close up too much."

I asked him to get the box containing all my medical gear, and addressing my helper, I said, "William, you will just have to take over," and I gave him a few directions concerning landmarks and the order in which he would pick them up, as an island was now well in sight. I then left the wheel to go to the maternity bay.

There were no real problems with the navigation, because everything went according to plan. However, because of the heavy rolling of the boat this was one of the most difficult deliveries that I had ever undertaken. Soon news spread the length of the ship that we had another passenger on board. A baby boy had been born and both mother and baby were well. As soon as I had everything attended to and was able to return to the wheelhouse, I found that William was just entering the Tora Pass, another little break from the rough seas.

We had to make two or three more calls to pick up

students, but the rest of the trip passed without incident except that all the students and passengers were very sick. Everyone certainly breathed a sigh of relief as we crossed the Vailala bar into calm waters. Mrs. Omohae informed me that she was going to call the baby Ura-Heni after the name of the boat. Both she and I recognized that we had seen God's hand at work once more.

Before I drop the anchor and turn off the navigation lights, I want to breathe a prayer of thankfulness and gratitude to my Captain by land, sea, and air.

Alma and I have left our hearts in New Guinea, the land of our adoption. My burden still remains as when I wrote the following verses some years ago when I was many days away in the mountains on an inland patrol.

# MISSIONARY'S PRAYER

There's something akin to the nomad
That flows deep within my veins,
When I think of the uncounted thousands
Held fast in the devil's iron chains.

In anguish they cry from the mountains,
Over rugged foot tracks and vales
*Good Master, no rest can reward me*
*While echo their pitiful wails.*

They challenge me too from the coast line,
Ten thousand and more voices call:
"Please tell us the true, living story
Of Jesus, who gave us His all."

Let me toil till my lifework is ended,
And then at the set of the sun
Meet those precious gems of the islands
And hear the words, "Elwyn, well done."